You're My Bambino!

FROM DYSFUNCTION TO DESTINY

Rob Gross

FAMILY LEGACY PUBLISHING

In an era when society is trying to convince us that fathers and mothers are not necessary, there needs to be a clear voice that declares truth-the truth that we desperately need healthy fathers and mothers! *You're My Bambino* is a dose of honesty about the essential nature of parenting. As you read this book, you will not be disappointed, as Rob has not only outlined for us the symptoms and diagnoses of inadequate parenting but also the cure for those who have become its victims. For those of you who are presently parenting or will soon be parenting, you will find guidelines in this book that will result in your children one day rising up and calling you blessed!

—PAUL L. COX
ASLAN'S PLACE, APPLE VALLEY, CALIFORNIA

In his book *You're My Bambino*, Rob Gross masterfully weaves together the topics of sonship, the orphan stronghold, and fatherhood under the banner of personal transformation. This book contains practical biblical principles and ministry guidelines for personal and small group Bible study. I highly recommend this book, as the author practices what he preaches! Rob's honesty and humility are revealed by his frank exposure of the attitudes of his heart. You will walk in the redemptive work of God's grace as you understand, reflect, and apply the truths contained in each chapter.

—DAVID ENOCH LEE
APOSTLE-PROPHET, CHRISTIAN INTERNATIONAL GLOBAL NETWORK

When it comes to helping people experience inner healing so they can experience the love of God, I know of no one better equipped than Rob Gross. Rob's new book, *You're My Bambino*, will help many people discover how to break free from the shame and dysfunction of their youth so they can become God's sons and daughters!

—DAVE BARR
SENIOR PASTOR, NEW HOPE WINDWARD CHRISTIAN FELLOWSHIP

Pastor Rob did a terrific job identifying the underlying problems in many families today in his description of the orphan spirit. More importantly, this book has the potential to guide individuals and families from a depressed and discouraged lifestyle to one destined for greatness. This book is a must read for every family.

—ALLEN CARDINES JR.
EXECUTIVE DIRECTOR, HAWAII FAMILY FORUM

You're My Bambino is about our heavenly Father calling His baby girls and boys to receive His love and healing. It is a book that will open people's hearts to the possibility that they can be healed by giving them steps to achieve freedom. As a therapist I believe this is a great training book that will equip counselors. Personally, I find Rob Gross' gift and anointing of teaching to be profound and humbling.

—MEMREY CASEY
LICENSED CLINICAL SOCIAL WORKER, CO-FOUNDER AND DIRECTOR OF IN HIS HOUSE HAWAII

Someone once said that sometimes you have to pray for the answer but sometimes we have to pray to be the answer. I sense that in Rob's new book, *You're My Bambino*, Rob is on to something here. His revelation about the orphan stronghold and how to break free from it is right on target. The Holy Spirit is using Rob to unlock spiritual treasures and principles that have been out of circulation for way too long. This is a God deal. My advice? Get this book. There is a stronghold of opportunity for you and you need to take a stronghold of it.

—DR. ED DELPH
NATIONSTRATEGY

Reaching your destiny is no easy task. *You're My Bambino* will help you to embrace God's absolute love for you! Once this is recognized, personal transformation can take place and you will be able to leave a legacy the way God intended. This book has motivated me to father my children, my clients, and my ministry! *You're My Bambino* is another great book about being a champion of posterity!

—DEL H. FUJINAKA
CO-FOUNDER, PERSONAL TRANSFORMATION INTERNATIONAL
CERTIFIED WEALTH STRATEGIST, PACIFIC RIM LEGACY CONSULTANTS, LLC

Rob Gross clearly outlines the deep hurts and wounds we all have encountered in our childhood. Countless number of people both believers and pre-believers are still living in bondage unable to fully live the abundant life that Jesus offers. But there's hope! Rob shares very simple and practical steps on how to identify these strongholds and pull them down! If we continue to be silent about the necessity for inner healing, not only will we perpetuate the bondage people are living in far into the future but we will also be guilty of preaching an incomplete Gospel.

—ELLIE KAPIHE
SENIOR PASTOR, WINDWARD MISSIONARY CHURCH

"See, I will send the prophet Elijah to you before that great and dreadful day of the LORD comes. He will turn the hearts of the parents to their children, and the hearts of the children to their parents" (Malachi 4:5–6). Pastor Rob Gross provides biblical and practical instructions that get to the heart of family. In the spirit of humility and transparency, Rob exhorts and provides hope to us that our families can be transformed. Reading and applying the truths in this book will bless your family and generations to come!

—MARK MORIMOTO
SENIOR PASTOR, KAKAAKO CHRISTIAN FELLOWSHIP

Freedom awaits you! Through *You're My Bambino* you will not only encounter God's heart for you but you will also receive fresh insights, revelations, and keys that will unlock a deeper intimacy with your heavenly Father and help you to love others well. Whether you are new in your journey with God or have been walking with Him for years, this book is a must read. I believe this will be a continual "go to" book for yourself as well as a powerful tool to minister to others God's truth and love. This is truly a masterpiece and legacy—a gift from the heart of God that will impact this generation and generations to come! *You're My Bambino* has transformed my life. Every child of the King needs to have this resource!"

—MICHELE OKIMURA
DIRECTOR, KINGDOM FAMILIES HAWAII

You're My Bambino is an incredible healing resource for individuals, families, and communities that integrate psychological and spiritual principles. Pastor Rob's clear instructions and explanations, authentic personal testimony, group discussion questions, and biblically-based prayers and methods create the space and opportunity for the healing and transforming work of Holy Spirit to operate. I am grateful that he has been inspired to publish this work and look forward to using this resource with my clients and church community. May all who have the courage to work through this resource be captivated by the Father's love *and* become His transforming agent to those around them.

—LISA N. ORIMOTO, PHD
CLINICAL PSYCHOLOGIST

Rob has done a masterful job at presenting the crucial issue of the power of fathers to either build or devastate a child's life. His personal journey from the challenges of dysfunction to the measure of wholeness he has gained is very rewarding. I was drawn into his journey and opened my own soul to further healing from the Lord. I can highly recommend you to journey with Rob to further wholeness.

—SAM WEBB
APOSTLE, EVERY NATION

The Apostle Paul writes, "For I do not understand my own actions. For I do not do what I want, but I do the very thing I hate" (Romans 7:15, ESV). If you don't understand your own actions and find yourself doing the very things you hate, then *You're My Bambino* is a must read. Pastor Rob Gross shares his own journey on how God brought him from victim to victory and the biblical truths that he learned along the way. I know of no other book that reads like a story but contains deep insights and truths to the hurts that keep us in bondage. If you want to be challenged, inspired, healed, and transformed, then this book is for you. Your life, your family, and your ministry will never be the same!

—DARYL YAMADA
SENIOR PASTOR, MILILANI MISSIONARY CHURCH AND FAMILY GATE
DIRECTOR, TRANSFORMATION HAWAII

You're My Bambino!
FROM DYSFUNCTION TO DESTINY

Copyright © 2014 by Rob Gross

Published by Family Legacy Publishing

FAMILY LEGACY
PUBLISHING

46-147 Nahiku Place
Kaneohe, Hawaii 96744

ISBN 979-8-6748-7391-4

Visit the author's website at: www.familylegacyinternational.org

You're My Bambino! available at www.amazon.com

Printed in the United States of America.

See, I will send you the prophet Elijah before that great and dreadful day of the Lord comes. He will turn the hearts of the fathers to their children, and the hearts of the children to their fathers; or else I will come and strike the land with a curse.
—Malachi 4:5–6

One day when the crowds were being baptized, Jesus himself was baptized. As he was praying, the heavens opened, and the Holy Spirit descended on him in the form of a dove. And a voice from heaven said, "You are my beloved Son, and I am fully pleased with you."
—Luke 3:21–22, nlt

I will not leave you as orphans. I will come to you.
—John 14:18

Humans give life to their children. Yet only God's Spirit can change you into a child of God.
—John 3:6, cev

Only those people who are led by God's Spirit are his children. God's Spirit doesn't make us slaves who are afraid of him. Instead, we become his children and call him our Father. God's Spirit makes us sure that we are his children.
—Romans 8:14–16, cev

And I will be your Father, and you will be my sons and daughters.
—2 Corinthians 6:18, nlt

His unchanging plan has always been to adopt us into his own family by bringing us to himself through Jesus Christ. And this gave him great pleasure.
—Ephesians 1:5, nlt

It is with great delight that I dedicate this book to my dear friends Paul and Donna Cox!

TABLE OF CONTENTS

Foreword

By Francis Oda
Chairman, Group 70 International
Senior Pastor, New Life Church Honolulu

Rob is a respected colleague and friend, yet this book surprised me. It tells, in intimate detail, of his journey as a physical and spiritual orphan to a true child of God. Yet, he neither realized that he was an orphan, angry with his deceased father and with God, nor that he had not truly accepted God's love as His adopted child.

Shocking for a pastor to admit? Not really since, as Rob's book shows, this is a common if not universal problem. As a pastor myself, I can affirm that many, if not most, Christians are spiritual orphans without realizing it. One can tell by our actions, our perceptions, and our hurting hearts. This starts with pastors, as Rob shows.

After sharing his personal epiphany, denying it all the way, Rob then translates his experiences into simple and practical steps for each of us. These steps begin with recognizing our orphanhood and then having the humility to ask others to help, extending forgiveness to our parents, and forgiving ourselves. This is first base.

Second base involves adoption after being healed to our earthly parents. Trust in authority must be restored and loving relationships with members of the Body of Christ must be nurtured with the result of fully grasping what it is to be adopted by Father God into His family!

Third base is then raising healthy children with the restored heart of a loved child who is a parent. This can also mean reconciling with children already grown; even if it means overcoming rejection. Rob's inspiring message is that it is not too late, and he shows us how to do it.

Reaching home plate—scoring—is achieving our God-given potential as His children. I believe that this is the heart cry of every believer. This is why this book is a must read. It's not just another inspiring story. Rob, in a humble and systematic manner, shows the way. Let's follow this path to the Father's home as legitimate children and heirs of His Kingdom.

1

Introduction

Surely the Sovereign Lord does nothing without **revealing his plan** to his servants the prophets.

—Amos 3:7

Do not be afraid, Zechariah; your prayer has been heard. Your wife Elizabeth will bear you a son, and you are to give him the name John. He will be a joy and delight to you, and, many will rejoice because of his birth, for he will be great in the sight of the Lord….Many of the people of Israel will he bring back to the Lord their God. And he will go on before the Lord, **in the spirit and power of Elijah**, to turn the hearts of the fathers to their children and the disobedient to the wisdom of the righteous—to make ready a people prepared for the Lord.

—Luke 1:13–17

But when he, the Spirit of truth, comes, he will guide you into all truth. He will not speak on his own; he will speak only what he hears, and he will tell you **what is yet to come**.

—John 16:13

God the Father Is Chasing You!

On a beautiful, sunny, seventy degree day in the East Bay, my wife, Barb, our twenty-month-old son Jordan, and I jumped into our car and traveled from Mill Valley to Berkeley, California, in search of a carpet for our new apartment.

Forty-five minutes later we arrived at the carpet store on University Avenue and went inside looking for a good deal. Barb began to look at some carpets rolled up against a chain-link fence and for a minute let go of Jordan's hand. Jordan peered through the chain-link fence and noticed a blue balloon attached to an A-frame sign on a median strip that divided the busy two-way traffic on University Avenue. Attracted by the balloon, Jordan wiggled his way through a small opening in the fence and began to walk onto the busiest street in Berkeley, California.

Noticing that Jordan was no longer by her side, Barb cried out, "Jordan, where are you?" In a moment of horror she saw Jordan step off the sidewalk and onto University Avenue. "Jordan, stop!" she screamed. Jordan looked back, grinned, and headed towards the balloon.

With my heart pounding I bolted through the store toward the front door. As I ran I prayed internally, "Please Lord, don't let him die!"

Expecting the worst, I witnessed a miracle. A female motorist noticed Jordan at the last second and came to a screeching stop right in front of him. The Lord had heard my prayer and saved my son!

Making my way out onto University Avenue, I snatched Jordan up into my arms; and with Barb behind me, we took him to our car. There, Barb and I cried over him for several minutes before scolding him for scaring us to death.

I share this story with you because this incident was and is a prophetic snapshot not only of a father (me) chasing after his son (Jordan) but a picture of God chasing His orphaned sons and daughters.

You're My Bambino has been written to those who have yet to experience the joy of knowing that they are God's precious sons or daughters. It is a book written to those who are spiritual orphans but don't know it. It is a book written for those who want to break free from the wounds of their childhood but haven't discovered how.

Words for the Hawaiian Islands and the Nations

In 1999 Chad Taylor posted the following prophetic word for the Hawaiian Islands. Fifteen years later Taylor's word is remarkably coming to pass.

A Word for the Hawaiian Islands

A time of confrontation is upon you.

I am confronting the things that have held your children in bondage for generations.

I am confronting the curses that have been permitted for centuries, that have blinded, maimed, and impaired you.

For in you is an Apostolic seed.

In you is the faith and wisdom to reveal My glory to the nations. Now know in this hour I have reserved you to reveal My power and My glory.

In you will be a reservoir of wisdom to sustain My people in the days to come. In you the nations will hear My heartbeat.

In you the orphan will find a home.

In you my will shall be revealed. For I have laid the Spirit of "wisdom and revelation" upon you. I will open the ancient gates and "the King of Glory will come in..."

Breakthroughs in science and technology will occur in your borders. It will be a sign of the spiritual breakthroughs that will mark the coming day of My church. It will mark the flood level of the rising waters of My glory upon the whole earth. You will be a forerunner to the greater works.

In your youth, in your children, there are the sounds of hunger, of thirst. Those that have been the most difficult will now run to your altars, they will run to your shelters, they will run to your outpouring and in-filling of My Spirit: To deliver, To set the captives free; To open the prison to those that are bound, and To bind up the broken hearted.

The principality of addiction and witchcraft is being undone. I am loosing its hold on the hearts of your people. They will once again by the thousands upon thousands declare, "What must we do to be saved!" This is the day of your salvation, the dawning of My visitation.[1]

That same year Jack and Trisha Frost of Shiloh Place Ministries also prophetically declared the coming move of the Holy Spirit in America. Incredibly, fifteen years later their word, like Chad Taylor's, is also coming to pass.

In 1999—Six Waves of Love to Roll across the Nations

In 1999, mighty waves of love will begin to roll across the nations in a greater magnitude than ever before. These waves will be the beginning of a paradigm (or way of thinking) shift of what we have known church life to be. They will come with such force that many who have not prepared their life with a spirit of brokenness and humility will be washed aside and their ministries will no longer have the effectiveness that they have had in the past. Others who may have been obscure and broken will quickly emerge to the forefront and will see cities impacted through a demonstration of anointing and power that is released through relationship, meekness, and love. (Matthew 11:29, 23:11–12)

There will be a set of at least six waves of love the Father will pour upon the earth.

(1) The first wave will flow over Christians who have been emotionally handicapped because they have not experienced the right kind of love. They are going to be saturated with the Father's unconditional love and acceptance. Fears of failure and rejection will be cast out by love. No longer will they compete and perform for love, identity, and acceptance but they will walk in a deeper sense of security, love and faith from a new found intimacy with the Father. (Isaiah 66:12–13)

(2) The second wave will be composed of humility and meekness and will anoint many leaders who have walked in positional authority of true spiritual fathers. Their life will exemplify Christ likeness, humility, meekness, and unconditional love. The anointing released through them will be based on intimacy and relationship, not just power, gifts, talents, and position. No longer will they struggle and weary themselves with raising up leaders but they will be at rest, fathering sons who will take the Father's healing love to the nations. Many fathers and sons will be set in their destinies to transform the nations in the Father's love. (1 Thessalonians 2:7–8)

(3) The third wave will release greater unity within the church than ever before. No longer competing for love, position, and identity but now resting on the Father's love and grace, pastors and different churches will begin to flow with one voice and one vision within their cities. Their heart's cry will be to make the Father's love known to their city and petty theological differences will fade away in the light of God's love. (Psalm 133)

(4) The fourth wave will bring the prodigal sons and daughters home. These are those who left the church because they have been so wounded by religion, those who felt they couldn't perform well enough and those who were so wounded in their youth and couldn't match up to church standards. They shall begin to return to the Father and to the spiritual fathers who now walk in humility and unconditional love. Joy will return to the church as it becomes a place where the 'heart of the fathers is restored to the heart of the sons, and the heart of the sons restored to the fathers'. (Malachi 4:5–6, Luke 15:20–24)

(5) Then, the fifth wave will bring in the lost. They will begin to see the difference the Father's love has made in Christian's lives. Before, their Christian work mates and family members were critical and judgmental of them but now love, servanthood, and acceptance flows from them. Their countenance is different. Their marriages are different. Being in a Christian's presence is no longer bad news to a lost person, but like a breath of fresh air. They begin to seek for the source of love and are led to the Father. A wave of revival begins to sweep the nations. (John 17:23)

(6) A whole paradigm shift in church life results. No longer will the church be an unsafe place for sinners and wounded people. No longer will many leave out of a need to be needed and to find identity, value, and self worth in ministry. No longer will many churches be performance based. The church will become the (My) Father's House, a place where the Father lives to meet the love needs of His children, and His children will be at rest, comforted in the Father's love. "The goal is for all of them to become one heart and mind, just as you, Father, are in me and I in you, so they might be one heart and mind in us. Then the world might believe that you in fact sent me. The same glory you gave me, I gave them, so they'll be as unified and together as we are—I in them and you in me. Then they'll be mature in this oneness, and give the godless world evidence that you've sent me and loved them in the same way you've loved me." (John 17:21–23, The Message)

WHAT TO EXPECT BEFORE EACH WAVE: We can expect to go through many relational and personal trials and testings in coming months. Many of the negative circumstances that will be going on around us will not be demonic, but the dealings of the Father, which are meant to break unbroken areas and to purify our motives so we find our need for utter dependence in Him and not in our gifts, talents, or position. Otherwise, the Spirit flowing out of us to others is blended and mixed with our unbroken soul. When we open our mouth, it is not pure but flows out of the impurity of a strong will or stubborn mind. Then our effectiveness to touch others with the Father's love is not hindered by a lack of anointing, but by the flow of impurities from our soul. (James 1:2–4)

Often, the greatest weakness we have is our inability to truly acknowledge our need for Him. Thus, the Father has us in the process of depleting our identity from being in our inheritance found in gifts, talents, and position (the prodigal son) so that He may bring us to the place of seeing that our greatest need is a deep personal intimate relationship with Him. It is difficult giving a gift to a person who has no need. We must first see our desperate need for the removal of the limitations of our soul that have hindered us from purely walking in the Father's unconditional love and acceptance. (John 15:4–5)

The brokenness the Father is leading us into is meant to reveal a supernatural revelation of His love deep in every area of need. Many of the troubles and trials we will experience are meant to bring us to a place of brokenness so the Father can pour forth His love deep within our soul. The measure of the Father's love being released in our life will depend upon how much we allow the Father to discipline, break, and transform us. (John 16:20–27)

During the trials, continue to stand firm in God's grace. Focus on the Father's love and acceptance for us. Nothing we do will make Him love us more and nothing we do will make Him love us less. We must not seek to blame others when things go wrong but allow the circumstance to be an opportunity for the Father's love to purify our soul and to cleanse us from all resentment and anger. Then we will begin to experience His wave of love flowing over us and washing away the fears, limitations, and hindrances of the past. (1 Peter 3:9–11)

In the Father's love, Jack and Trisha Frost[2]

We are entering one of the most exciting seasons in church history as the Lord is transitioning His church worldwide from a global orphanage into a family of sons and daughters. As this transformation evolves, we the church will be able to recognize what our Father is doing (see John 5:19) and advance the Kingdom of God. As you read this book, may the Holy Spirit show you that you are His precious bambino!

SECTION I

BREAKING FREE FROM THE ORPHAN STRONGHOLD

1

You're God's Bambino!

*About Benjamin he said: "Let the beloved of the LORD rest secure in him, for he shields him all day long, and the one the LORD loves **rests** between his shoulders."*
—DEUTERONOMY 33:12

Resting Between Your Father's Shoulders

The cry of God's heart is for you to rest in His love! His deepest longing is for you to know Him as your Daddy! His greatest desire is to "Father" you!

My favorite childhood picture remains on top of a bookshelf in my eighty-eight-year-old mother's bedroom. In this picture I am clinging to my father's back while he and my mother are leaning into each other head-to-head. In this photo my face reveals a little boy content and at rest between his father's shoulders.

No family is perfect. The reality is that our most painful memories and experiences are often traceable to hurtful events while growing up in our families. This book will help you to break free from the structures, mind-sets, and beliefs that have blinded and blocked you from knowing God as your Father. This book will also address the importance of family and how God's end-time revival plan is to heal our nation by healing our families.

Three Powerful Words!

In the year 2001 a contingent of church leaders from Hawaii attended Harvest Evangelism's annual nation transformation conference in Buenos Aires, Argentina. Among the many pastors and marketplace leaders traveling to Argentina, were my friends Dean Fujishima and Cal Chinen.

During one of the conference breaks Dean, Cal, and I ventured out into the heart of Buenos Aires' shopping district to search for the highly prized Argentine leather jackets. As we walked along window shopping from store to store, a prophetically gifted woman from evangelist Carlos Annocondia's ministry bumped into us and began to speak words of encouragement over us. She spoke first a powerful word to Dean about his future ministry. As she did so, tremendous envy rose in my heart. At this time in my life, I was dealing with deep insecurity but was too proud to admit it. After all, I was a pastor. Pastors should be strong, not insecure and certainly not envious of other pastors.

You're God's Bambino!

After speaking a word of encouragement to Dean, the woman turned and pointed her finger at me. I thought to myself, "Yes, Lord! Tell me all the great things You plan to do through me like You're going to do through Dean. This is why I have come to Argentina!" To my great disappointment, however, the woman said to me, "You're God's bambino!" motioning back and forth like a mother holding her baby. Tears began to roll down my face as the Lord's presence came upon me. Cal Chinen, who was at my side, exclaimed, "Wow, Rob, what an awesome word!" I thought to myself, "What a junk word! Everyone is God's baby. I know this already and I don't need this! I need a word that's going to tell me about the great things God is going to do in my ministry!"

As I look back to that time in Buenos Aires, I now realize that the Lord had deposited into my spirit something He wanted me to understand but did not grasp: I am His baby! I am His child! I am His favored son!

These three words, you're My bambino, are the words that have inspired me to write this book. These three words came from heaven through an Argentine woman I didn't even know. God spoke to me because I needed the revelation that He is my Father and I am His son!

Old Mind-sets Die Hard

I returned from Argentina eight days later exhausted and drained. At this point I didn't understand what God had spoken to me in Argentina about being His baby, so I willed my way through my tiredness and continued to try and build my life and ministry out of my own strength. The Bible makes it clear in John 6:63

that this kind of approach doesn't work:

> The spirit can make life. Sheer muscle and willpower don't make any-
> thing happen.
>
> —JOHN 6:63, THE MESSAGE

In this passage, Jesus was speaking to the Jews, who for generations had attempted to be right with God by keeping the Law—an impossible task! God wants us to receive the revelation today that our lives don't have to be complicated and difficult. He wants us to understand that we don't have to go through this life as orphans—those whose lives are built upon sheer muscle and willpower.

In chapter two, "Understanding the Orphan Stronghold," we will explore what it means to live a life without God the Father.

Thoughts to Ponder

Chapter One

1. The cry of God's heart is for you to rest in His love! His deepest longing is for you to know Him as your Daddy! His greatest desire is to "Father" you!

2. No family is perfect. The reality is that our most painful memories and experiences are often traceable to hurtful events while growing up in our families.

3. God wants us to know that our lives don't have to be complicated and difficult. He wants us to understand that we don't have to go through this life on our own (see John 6:63).

Small Group Discussion Questions
Chapter One

1. Share briefly what it was like to grow up in your family.

2. Read Deuteronomy 33:12.

3. Does this verse speak to you or is it a foreign concept? Why or why not?

4. Which of the following words describe your relationship with God? (1) Intimate, (2) Neutral, (3) Distant. Why?

5. Pray for one another as the Lord leads.

2 | Understanding the Orphan Stronghold

No, I will not abandon you as **orphans**—*I will come to you.*
—JOHN 14:18, NLT

Orphaned at Fifteen

During the middle of August 1974, my parents and I traveled to the island of Kauai for a family vacation at the Princeville Hotel and Resort. To this day I have vivid memories of that special week when my father and I played golf together every day on Robert Trent Jones' stunning twenty-seven hole championship golf course. I was only fifteen at the time and becoming a man. That week I felt a tremendous sense of connection with my dad as we talked, laughed, and enjoyed the beauty of Kauai together.

A week later after returning home to Oahu, I participated in football drills across the Ala Wai Canal with the rest of Iolani's Junior Varsity high school football squad as we prepared for the 1975 season opener. Little did I know that I was about to lose my father.

I clearly remember the night my mother informed me that my dad was having severe chest pains and needed to go to the hospital. As I walked into my parents' bedroom, I saw my father sitting up at the edge of his bed clutching his chest. His face said it all—he was battling for his life!

That night my dad underwent open heart surgery at Queen's Hospital. I visited him in intensive care as he lay motionless under heavy sedation. I cried as I touched his arm and told him that I loved him. I would never see him again.

That night my mom and I spent the night at her sister's home. The next morning I was awakened by my Aunt Yoshie. She hugged and kissed me as she

18

told me that my father had just passed away. Pain seared through my soul as I wept uncontrollably—**nothing could comfort me!**

A week later my mother and I said goodbye to my dad at his funeral service at Punchbowl National Cemetery. Although I remember little about that day, I do remember that I refused to cry.

Every orphan carries within his heart a father or mother wound or both leading him to believe that he does not belong—that no one cares about him and that he has no inheritance!

What Is the Orphan Stronghold?

The word *orphan* comes from the Greek word *orphanos*, which literally means "comfortless." When Jesus told His twelve disciples that He would not leave them as orphans (John 14:18), He knew they would feel the sting of His absence after He went back to the Father. Although Jesus knew His spiritual sons would be unable to comprehend what He meant at that moment, He also knew that He would send His Spirit, enabling them to cry "Abba Father!" (Rom. 8:15–16). The Greek word for Holy Spirit is *Paraclete*, which means "Comforter." Jesus had made provision for His spiritual sons to be "comforted" so they would not be hindered by the orphan stronghold.

Although the orphan stronghold has many faces and variations, those who have it have one thing in common—core pain. Every orphan carries within his heart a father or mother wound, or both, leading him to believe that he does not belong—that no one cares about him and that he has no inheritance!

An *orphan* is an individual who has lost one or both parents. This definition, while accurate, is incomplete because one can be "orphaned" without losing one or both parents. How is this possible? A simple definition of the term *stronghold* gives us the answer. A stronghold is a mind-set impregnated with false conclusions or lies that have "strong hold" on the way a person "perceives" God, themselves, and others. The orphan stronghold is a "mind-set" that has been shaped by disappointments, rejection (real or perceived), hurts, lack of nurture, and the absence of parental instruction. At its deepest level, the orphan stronghold is a "wall of protection" fueled by lies that a person has unconsciously built around his heart to never be hurt again.

Anger and Insecurity: The Fruit of My Father's Death

After telling my father how much I loved him, I left the intensive care unit and

19

walked to the Queen's Hospital parking lot to wait for my mother, who was making arrangements with my aunt for us to spend the night at her home. As I waited for my mother, I pleaded with God to spare my father's life.

As I mentioned at the beginning of this chapter, my aunt woke me to tell me that my dad had died. Although I cannot recall thinking, "This is God's fault," I surely concluded this; because years later I rejected those God sent to share the Gospel with me.

I was deeply hurt because I believed that both my father and heavenly Father had abandoned me! Now that my father was gone, who would explain what it meant to be a man? Who would help me navigate my way through life? It was during this season that tremendous insecurity and anger crept into my soul.

Performance Drivenness

Although my mom never intended to wound me, the hurts she sustained during her childhood affected me. My mom, who is presently eighty-eight, was raised by parents who immigrated to the United States from Japan. Both of her parents were hard working people who wanted to provide a better life for their children. Yet, they wounded my mother, albeit unintentionally. My grandfather was a very proud and stoic man from an aristocratic family. He never received affection from his father and therefore could not give any affection to my mother—or speak any words of affirmation over her. My grandmother, on the other hand, was a kind, happy woman who nurtured her children. Like many Asian parents, she expected my mother to perform at a high level academically in order to bring honor to the family. My grandfather's lack of affirmation and my grandmother's academic expectations led my mother to conclude that if she wanted to be loved she had to earn it.

As a boy I grew up hearing about my mother's academic achievements, as she was the class valedictorian of her high school and went on to attend Yale University. Doing well was not an option in my mother's family; it was mandatory! It was no surprise that I believed that acceptance and affirmation were tied to performance. This lie was reinforced at the age of ten when my grandfather wanted all of his seven grandchildren, including me, to participate in a writing contest. He told us that he would award money to the top four finishers.

Encouraged by our parents, each of us wrote ten-page essays and handed them in to our grandfather to review. Two weeks later he called a family gathering and named the top four contestants. To my great relief I finished in fourth place and received $25. Three of my cousins, obviously, did not receive any money.

Among them was my cousin Steve, who was told by my grandfather in front of all of us that he wrote a very poor paper. My aunt and uncle stormed out the room in anger. I felt badly for my cousin! I had no idea how family experiences like this were building performance-oriented structures into my soul.

Family expectations and performance-oriented values fuel within children a drivenness to succeed because they want to be loved and affirmed. Performance-oriented individuals struggle with orphan mind-sets because they believe that love, praise, and affirmation must be earned instead of received. Orphans believe that if they perform poorly or let others down, they will be rejected. Because of this lie, performance-oriented individuals find it difficult to rest, and they believe they have to "help" God get things done.

A Lost Childhood

In addition to being performance oriented, I became "parentally inverted." This came about as the result of my father's absence. Because of this, my mother turned to me for advice and emotional support. I quickly shifted from being an adolescent to filling the role of husband. I lost my childhood and took adult responsibilities upon my fifteen-year-old shoulders. Consequently, I became an even more driven, responsible, angry, and insecure individual.

Orphans in the Bible

The Bible is full of stories about orphans. In this section I would like to examine the historical background of three orphans: Ishmael, Absalom, and Esther.

Ishmael, Son of Abraham

Genesis 21:8–21 describes the story of how Abraham orphaned Ishmael:

> The child grew and was weaned, and on the day Isaac was weaned Abraham held a great feast. But Sarah saw that the son whom Hagar the Egyptian had borne to Abraham was mocking, and she said to Abraham, "Get rid of that slave woman and her son, for that slave woman's son will never share in the inheritance with my son Isaac." The matter distressed Abraham greatly because it concerned his son. But God said to him, "Do not be so distressed about the boy and your maidservant. Listen to whatever Sarah tells you, because it is through Isaac that your offspring will be reckoned. I will make the son of the maidservant into a nation also, because he is your offspring." Early the next morning Abraham took some food and a skin of water and gave them to Hagar. He set them on her shoulders and then sent her off with the boy. She

went on her way and wandered in the desert of Beersheba. When the water in the skin was gone, she put the boy under one of the bushes. Then she went off and sat down nearby, about a bowshot away, for she thought, "I cannot watch the boy die." And as she sat there nearby, she began to sob. God heard the boy crying, and the angel of God called to Hagar from heaven and said to her, "What is the matter, Hagar? Do not be afraid; God has heard the boy crying as he lies there. Lift the boy up and take him by the hand, for I will make him into a great nation." Then God opened her eyes and she saw a well of water. So she went and filled the skin with water and gave the boy a drink. God was with the boy as he grew up. He lived in the desert and became an archer. While he was living in the Desert of Paran, his mother got a wife for him from Egypt.

Ishmael and his mother Hagar were sent out into the wilderness of Beersheba by Abraham. Ishmael, only a teenager at the time, lost his father, Abraham, his half-brother, Isaac, and the security that he and his mother enjoyed while living under his father's protection. Ishmael became an orphan overnight with no father to guide his life.

To make matters more complicated, Ishmael's mother, Hagar, and her mistress, Sarah, had had a stormy relationship that deteriorated because Sarah was unable to bear children. In a moment of poor judgment, Sarah rushed ahead of God's timing and persuaded her husband to have sexual relations with Hagar in an effort to produce Abraham's offspring. Ishmael was conceived and Sarah became jealous of Hagar and began to treat her harshly! (See Genesis 16:1–6.) Hagar, now displaced from Abraham's camp headed into the wilderness a broken, angry woman who blamed her mistress for influencing Abraham's decision to send her and her son away.

Imagine for a moment what Ishmael must have felt as his father told him to leave his tent. Imagine the flood of emotions that seared through him knowing that he would never again feel his father's embrace, hear his voice, or receive his guidance. Imagine what he must have felt when he realized he would never see his brother again. Imagine what Ishmael must have thought as he watched his mother weep uncontrollably. What did Ishmael conclude as the result of these traumatic experiences? What lies did he believe about himself, his father, his mother, and his brother? What did he think about his father's God? And how did this painful experience shape his future? His legacy? Genesis 25:17–18 provides a clue of how Ishmael was impacted:

> Altogether, Ishmael lived a hundred and thirty-seven years. He breathed his last and died, and he was gathered to his people. His de-

scendants settled in the area from Havilah to Shur, near the border of Egypt, as you go to Asshur. And [he] lived in **hostility** [defiance] toward all [his] brothers.

Absalom, Son of David

Second Samuel 3:2–3 tells us that Absalom was born in Hebron. He was the son of David and Maacah, the daughter of Talmai, king of Geshur. The Bible doesn't say much about Absalom for several chapters. Instead, it details the events of his father's reign. During this period of his life, David was busy fighting the house of King Saul (2 Sam. 3:1). Like a modern day Steve Jobs, he found little time for his children. Whether it was warring against the Philistines, bringing the ark of the covenant back to Jerusalem, or planning to build a temple for the Lord, David was consumed with work. His workaholic lifestyle eventually proved costly for three of his adult children. Sadly, David also committed adultery with Bathsheba and had her husband, Uriah, killed (see 2 Samuel 11:1–24). Without knowing it, the king of Israel had unleashed a river of toxic waste upon his children's children (see Exodus 20:5).

In 2 Samuel 13 we read where David's son Amnon raped and then shamed his half-sister Tamar. It is at this point that we read again about Absalom, Tamar's older brother. Enraged by his half-brother's terrible actions he commanded his servants to kill his brother (v. 28).

What a tragedy it is when a father exposes his children to the strongholds of sexual impurity and murder! What a tragedy when a dad is so busy that he doesn't spend time to with his children! What a tragedy when a father doesn't impart godly values to his children! What a tragedy when a father fails to discipline his kids!

When a father does not discipline or instruct his son or daughter, they will be prone to rebellion!

And, when David thought life couldn't get any worse, his son Absalom rebelled against him and usurped his kingdom. In 2 Samuel 15 we read how Absalom seduced the people of Israel and took his father's throne. Because David had failed to discipline his son for killing his half-brother and refused to confront him, Absalom believed he could get away with anything. He had no boundaries and no respect for authority!

When a father does not discipline or instruct his son or daughter, they will be prone to rebellion. Absalom was an orphan son who did not know his father, his father's ways, and, most of all, his father's God.

Esther, Queen of Persia

Esther 2:7 reveals that the eventual Queen of Persia was also an orphan:

Mordecai had a cousin named Hadassah, whom he had brought up because **she had neither father nor mother**. This girl, who was also known as Esther, was lovely in form and features, and Mordecai had taken her as his own daughter when her father and mother died.

Although Esther was an orphan, she was "fathered" by Mordecai. We cannot overlook this seemingly small detail of Esther's life. If Mordecai had not poured into Esther, she probably would not have become the queen of Persia and been able to save the Jewish people from extermination. There can be no doubt that because Mordecai had "fathered" Esther she became a woman who had the character to be a queen!

Ishmael and Absalom are examples of how a father's absence can alter a child's destiny. Esther, however, is an example of how a child's future can be shaped and prepared to achieve their life purpose when a father or father figure pours into them!

To review, the orphan stronghold is a mind-set impregnated with lies that has a "strong hold" on the way a person perceives God, himself, and others. It is a fortress of lies. It is a wall of protection around a person's heart that keeps them from experiencing the fullness of God's love and blessings.

Famous Orphans

In addition to biblical orphans, there are thousands of examples of famous or recognizable orphans in American society. Some of these individuals grew up in orphanages, some in foster homes, and most were abandoned by one or both their parents.

Marilyn Monroe

Perhaps the most famous orphan of the twentieth century was Marilyn Monroe. Monroe was born in Los Angeles on June 1, 1926, as Norma Jeane Mortenson. Monroe's birth certificate names her father as Martin Edward Mortensen. Monroe's mother, Gladys Pearl Baker, was mentally and financially unable to care for Norma Jeane and placed her with foster parents until she was seven. Later Gladys Baker's best friend, Grace McKee, became Norma Jeane's guardian until she married two years later. At the age of nine, Norma Jeane was placed in an orphanage and then a succession of different foster homes. In 1937 Grace McKee reconnected with Norma Jeane and took her into her new husband's home. This arrangement went terribly wrong, as McKee's husband attempted on several occasions to sexually assault Norma Jeane. Fearing for Norma Jeane's safety, McKee sent Monroe to live with her great aunt Olive (Brunings). This new living situation also proved to be traumatic, as one of Olive's sons sexually assaulted her too.[1]

Marilyn Monroe's childhood is an example of a literal orphan. With neither father nor mother present in her life to raise her in a stable environment, she grew up longing to be loved. Her life was characterized by looking for love in multiple relationships, drugs, alcohol, and personal achievement.

Mike Tyson

Mike Tyson was the undisputed heavyweight champion and holds the record as the youngest boxer to win the WBC, WBA and IBF world heavyweight titles.[2] Tyson is also widely known for his angry outbursts, his abusive behavior towards his ex-wife Robin Givens and being jailed for raping a beauty queen contestant.[3]

Born in Brooklyn New York in 1966 Tyson experienced a difficult childhood. Tyson's father, Jimmy Kirkpatrick, abandoned his family when Tyson was only two leaving his mother, Lorna Smith Tyson to care for them on her own.[4]

By the time Tyson reached the age of thirteen he had been arrested thirty-eight times. Three years later his mother died leaving him in the care of boxing manager and trainer Cus D'Amato.[5]

Tyson's unstable life is traceable to not having a father in his early years and losing his mother as an adolescent.

Lindsay Lohan

Lindsay Lohan was born on July 2, 1986. She is an American actress, pop singer, and model. She began her career as a child fashion model before making her motion picture debut in Disney's 1998 remake of the *Parent Trap* at the age of eleven. Lohan gained further fame between 2003 and 2005 with leading roles in the films *Freaky Friday, Mean Girls*, and *Herbie: Fully Loaded.*[6]

In recent years Lohan's career has been interrupted by several DUI (driving under the influence) incidents, multiple visits to drug rehabilitation facilities, and lost movie deals and nationally televised appearances in court for shoplifting.[7]

Lohan's struggles are traceable to her parents' turbulent marital history.

Married in 1985 Michael and Dina Lohan separated several times before finally getting a divorce in 2005.[8]

Lohan co-wrote and performed a song called "Confessions of a Broken Heart" in 2005. This song can be viewed on Youtube.com and reveals the hurt Lindsay felt when her father left her home. The lyrics reveal the heart of an orphan abandoned by her father:

> I wait for the postman to bring me a letter
> And I wait for the good Lord to make me feel better
> And I carry the weight of the world on my shoulders
> A family in crisis that only grows older
>
> Why'd you have to go?
> Why'd you have to go?
> Why'd you have to go?
>
> Daughter to father, daughter to father
> I am broken but I am hoping
> Daughter to father, daughter to father
> I am cryin', a part of me's dying'
> And these are, these are
> The confessions of a broken heart
>
> And I wear all your old clothes, your polo sweater
> I dream of another you, one who would never
> Never leave me alone to pick up the pieces
> A daddy to hold me, that's what I needed
>
> So why'd you have to go?
> Why'd you have to go?
> Why'd you have to go?
>
> Daughter to father, daughter to father
> I don't know you, but I still want to
> Daughter to father, daughter to father
> Tell me the truth, did you ever love me?
> Cause these are, these are
> The confessions of a broken heart, of a broken heart
>
> I love you
> I love you
> I love you
> I, I, I, I love you
>
> Daughter to father, daughter to father
> I don't know you, but I still want to

Daughter to father, daughter to father
Tell me the truth, did you ever love me?
These are the confessions of a broken heart
Oh yeah

I wait for the postman to bring me a letter[9]

Marilyn Monroe, Mike Tyson, and Lindsay Lohan are three examples of celebrities who, although incredibly successful, have struggled from the effects of not being parented.

In chapter three, "How Do We Get Orphaned?" we will learn how fathers misrepresent God the Father to their children, causing them to relate to Him not as sons and daughters but as orphans.

Thoughts to Ponder

Chapter Two

1. The word orphan comes from the Greek word *orphanos* which literally means "comfortless," while the Greek word for the Holy Spirit means "Comforter."

2. A stronghold is a mind-set impregnated with false conclusions or lies that have a "strong hold" on the way you "perceive" God, yourself, and others.

3. The orphan stronghold is an "outlook" that has been shaped by your disappointments, hurts, and lack of nurture. It is at the deepest level, a "wall of protection" that you have unconsciously built around your heart to ensure that you will never be hurt again.

4. Ishmael lost his father, Abraham, his half-brother, Isaac, and the security that he and his mother enjoyed while under his father's protection. Ishmael became an orphan overnight with no father to guide his life (Gen. 21:14).

5. When a father does not discipline or instruct his son or daughter, they will eventually become a rebel. Absalom was an orphan son who did not know his father, his father's ways, and (most of all) his father's God.

6. If Mordecai had not poured into Esther, she probably would not have become the queen of Persia and been able to save the Jewish people from extermination.

7. Esther is an example of how a child's future can be shaped and prepared to achieve their life purpose when a father figure pours into their life!

8. Marilyn Monroe, Mike Tyson, and Lindsay Lohan are examples of celebrities who, although incredibly successful, have struggled from the effects of not being parented.

Small Group Discussion Questions

Chapter Two

1. Read John 14:18.

2. What is an orphan? a stronghold? the orphan stronghold?

3. Can you identify any orphan characteristics in yourself?

4. Identify an event where you felt rejected by your parents (or less valued).

5. Read Genesis 21:8–21. What do you think Ishmael thought about himself after his father asked him to leave? And how, from that day forward, do you think Ishmael related to father figures or persons in authority? Do you struggle with authority figures? If so, why?

6. Read 2 Samuel 15. Based on this chapter, why do you think Absalom turned against his father David?

7. Read Esther 2:7. Although Esther did not have a father, she rose to great heights because Mordecai poured into her life! Who has poured into your life and what difference has their mentorship had on you?

8. Pray for one another as the Spirit leads.

How Do We Get Orphaned?

3

*For I have come to you **representing** my Father, and you refuse to welcome me, even though you readily accept others who represent only themselves.*
—JOHN 5:43, NLT

Orphan Mind-Sets

Over the years I have counseled men and women for a variety of different issues. From these interactions it is my observation that no individual is exempt from some level of orphan thinking. I have listed below some of **the mind-sets** that orphans believe.

- God doesn't love me!
- I am not worthy to receive anything from God!
- I don't belong in God's family!
- I am a bad person!
- I am messed up!
- No one cares about me!
- My feelings don't matter!
- No one wants to be my friend!
- I don't have what it takes to be a man!
- I am not an attractive woman!
- There is no such thing as a happy family!
- The best way to avoid hurt is to isolate myself from others!
- Significant people in my life will not be there for me when I need their help!
- I am valuable to others only for what I can do for them!
- Even when I give my best it is not good enough!

- I am what I am! I cannot change!
- I am all alone!
- Authority figures cannot be trusted![1]

Orphans Guard Their Hearts

On February 10, 2008, my son Jordan and I arrived at Los Angeles International Airport to check in our luggage and verify our fourteen-hour EL AL flight to Tel Aviv, Israel. Little did we know that we were about to experience the intricacies of Israeli security.

From standing in line to check in to finally boarding our plane we were asked questions, patted down, X-rayed, checked and re-checked. It was by far the strictest and most thorough security process I have ever experienced!

To cite a specific example during this time, my guitar was put through a high-tech X-ray machine. This was not unusual until prior to boarding the flight when my name was called through the airport intercom. I made my way toward the boarding tunnel and was escorted to another area where I was asked to identify my guitar. After verifying that it was my guitar, I was then asked to open it so security personnel could examine it. Once they re-checked it and were satisfied it didn't contain a bomb, they put it on the plane.

With all the terroristic acts the Israelis have experienced, no one can blame them for being overly cautious. Orphans are like Israeli security because they are extremely careful not to allow anyone to hurt them again.

Computer Programs of the Soul

Orphans build "walls of protection" around their hearts by making inner directives referred to in the counseling community as inner vows. Inner vows are computer programs of the soul, which, when subconsciously made, "protect" a person from being hurt in the future. Some examples are:

- I will **never** be like my dad...like my mom!
- I will **be a far better parent** than my dad was...than my mom was!
- I will **never** let anyone in authority tell me what to do!
- I will **never** let an authority figure hurt me again!
- I will **never** trust anyone in authority!
- I will **never** be accepted for who I really am!
- I will **not** allow anyone to get close to me because if I do they will reject me!
- I will **reject** others before they reject me!

- I will **never** be successful!
- I will **always** be lonely!
- I will **always** have to figure out how to do things on my own!
- I will **never** be able to give or receive love or have a satisfying relationship with anyone!
- I will **always** be on guard as to what I say to others or those words will be used against me!

Orphan Characteristics

As previously noted, orphans believe specific lies about themselves and others. They also, as you have learned, carefully "guard" their hearts. Generally individuals who carry orphan structures can be identified by the following behaviors and characteristics.

Orphans:

- are always on the lookout for something bigger and beter!
- are convinced that no one cares about them!
- get easily rejected and offended!
- don't believe they have a future!
- don't feel like they belong!
- don't need others as they are fiercely independent (they have difficulty receiving help from others)!
- don't trust authority figures!
- have a "survivalist" outlook (they look out for theselves)!
- have difficulty being transparent!
- are lonely, afraid, and insecure!
- are uncomfortable in the presence of an anointed spiritual father!
- are unable to draw close to God, hear His voice, or connect with their heavenly Father's family—the church!
- are very "soulish" because their spirit man is hiding or asleep!
- are unable to put roots down in a church family!
- are unable to overcome challenges and conflict!
- are unable to nurture others!
- use others for self gain!
- withdraw quickly when they get hurt (they have an "I'm out of here" spirit)!
- believe they have to uphold a false image of themselves to

others lest they be rejected!

An Unexpected Gang Fight

One of our youth leaders shared that, while leading a Bible study at our church office one evening, he heard shouting outside. Looking out the window across the street, he saw a group of young men and women engaged in an all-out brawl. He ran outside shouting, "The cops are coming! The cops are coming! Get out of here! The cops are coming!" His attempt to break up the fight did not succeed, as the young men continued to fight.

As I thought about this incident, I wondered if the parents of these high schoolers knew where their sons and daughters were that evening or if they even cared. I wondered what kind of families these high schoolers came from and if anyone was guiding or helping them navigate their way through life. And I wondered, how could a gang fight happen in my city where violent behavior has been the exception, not the rule?

I believe that whatever the stronghold is in your city or region, it is traceable to instability in the home. Unstable families weaken cities, societies, and nations. Conversely, transformed families transform cities, societies, and nations!

Abused at the Age of Sixteen

In the same season that the gang fight broke out across from our office, the Lord brought to our church a middle-aged, unemployed, single mother. I asked this woman if she was would share her story with me. I was particularly interested in discovering why a gifted, intelligent person like her was living below the poverty line.

With tears streaming down her face, she shared that her father had physically and verbally abused her at the age of sixteen. Not willing to be mistreated any longer, she left home vowing never to return. Decades later she found herself living in low-income housing, unable to pay her rent, and still estranged from her father.

Punished for Not Performing Up to Expectations

A twenty-three-year-old man recounted to me how his father established goals for him when he played Pop Warner football as a boy. Because he played on the defensive line, his father told him that he needed to sack (tackle) the quarterback at least once per game. Later, when he began to play high school football, his dad informed him that his sack quota had gone up to two per game. These goals weren't bad; but when he failed to achieve them, his father physically abused him by making him sit in the family car with the heater turned up with his football gear still on. This led this young man to turn to drugs and alcohol to kill the pain from his father's abuse.

One of Ten Children

I listened to a fifty-year-old man tell me about his thirty-four year battle with drug addiction. As he shared his story, it was evident why he had turned to drugs at the age of sixteen. As the youngest of ten children, he was left to figure out life on his own. He had no parental boundaries, no discipline, and no father in his life. His struggles were compounded as his mother was not his father's wife but his mistress. This led him to seek approval and acceptance from the wrong crowd, which plunged him into the world of addiction and drug dealing. After being told by his doctor that his heart was failing due to drug abuse, he began to realize that he, his wife, and his son were paying a heavy price for the habit he clung to so tenaciously.

Hurtful Parenting

Whether a gang member involved in a brawl, a single mom struggling to make ends meet, a high school boy trying to kill his pain, or a married man addicted to methamphetamines, there seems to be a common theme that explains why people struggle—hurts inflicted by their parents. I thank God that He is turning the hearts of parents back to their children and vice versa!

Representing the Father

John 5:43 tells us "For I [Jesus] have come to you **representing my Father**, and you refuse to welcome me, even though you readily accept others who represent only themselves" (NLT). This verse tells us that Jesus came to represent His heavenly Father. In his letter to the Colossians, Paul stated that Jesus "is the **image** of the invisible God" (Col. 1:15, NKJV). Like John, Paul made it clear that if you want to know what God is like, examine the life of Jesus.

The primary calling of every parent is to "represent" the nature and character of God to their children. This call, however, was severely affected when Adam and Eve disobeyed God in the Garden of Eden and ate the fruit from the tree of the knowledge of good and evil (see Genesis 3:5–7). From that time forward every father and mother has been self focused instead of God focused. This has created all kinds of challenges. Down through history every parent has been unable to accurately represent the Father to their children the way the Father originally intended.

In his book *Experiencing Father's Embrace*, Jack Frost identifies six specific ways fathers misrepresent Father God to their children.

- The **Good** father
- The **Absent** father
- The **Abusive** father
- The **Authoritarian** father
- The **Passive** father
- The **Performance-oriented** father

These father flaws, Frost states, are the lenses through which children view and understand God the Father.[2]

The Good Father

As I've shared in chapter two, my father was a good dad. I loved and cherished him with all my heart. Although strict at times, he wisely counterbalanced the discipline I deserved with a lot of praise and affection. Yet, when he suffered an unexpected heart attack and died, he unintentionally wounded my heart.

Because my father was such a wonderful dad, I stuffed the anger I felt towards him for abandoning me. How could I be angry at him? After all, he was the best dad a kid could have!

I later discovered that I was angry not only at my father for leaving me but also angry at my heavenly Father because I had believed the lie that He had taken my dad. This anger manifested off and on for over two decades, some at friends and at other times total strangers. But when I began to rage at my wife, I knew something was radically wrong in my soul. I will share later in chapter six how the Lord set me free from anger.

"Good" dads who wound their children are hard to forgive; because their children not only want to protect their good names, they also find it terribly difficult to face the pain of what their fathers did or did not do for them. Furthermore, the hurt that good dads unintentionally inflict upon their kids end up shaping their children's view of their heavenly Father. In my case, I was closed to God for years, even though He sent people to tell me about Jesus on many occasions.

The Absent Father

Another misrepresentation of God by earthly fathers is the "absent" dad. Absent fathers simply are not around for their children while they are growing up. They miss the small, yet very important, moments like bedtime stories, sporting events, extracurricular activities, birthdays, etc. A man in our congregation shared with me that, although his dad was an excellent provider, he rarely saw him because his father worked at night. His dad was at home and slept during the day while he was at school. Not surprisingly, this man said that he found it easy to have a relationship with Jesus but could not connect or experience God's (the Father's) love.

Those who had absent fathers also seem to have the most difficulty pinpointing any significant ways their ways their dads hurt them during their childhood. Their wounds are not traceable to a moment or series of events but to a childhood bereft of contact and instruction.

The Abusive Father

"Abusive" fathers, another misrepresentation of God, lead their children to conclude that the abuse they received was their fault. A pastor shared with me that her dad constantly rejected her by ridiculing her looks and making other nasty comments about her throughout her childhood. He told her that he had to marry her mother because he had gotten her pregnant. Her father deeply resented this and blamed her for it. For years, before God healed her, she believed that she deserved her father's verbal abuse. Abusive fathers also shape a child's understanding of God via "the fear of punishment." Because of this, God is someone to be greatly feared instead of someone who is unconditionally loving and merciful.

The Authoritarian Father

"Authoritarian" fathers are very rule oriented and demand prompt obedience from their children. This father type plants the seeds of religiosity and legalism into their children's hearts through the ongoing threat of punishment. This causes their children to become highly critical and judgmental, not only of others but of themselves. Sadly, children who have been raised under "the roof of legalism" perceive Christianity as a harsh religion full of rules and regulations instead of an intimate relationship with their heavenly Daddy.

The Passive Father

"Passive" fathers, like "absent" fathers, are not present for their children but in a different way. Although at home, they do not talk to their children and are typically not involved in their lives. Passive fathers often leave the running of the household to their wives, including making most if not all of the decisions including disciplining the children.

Passive fathers are typically unaware that they have injured their children by portraying the Father as passive when He, according to the Bible, is continually "active" in the lives of His children. Passive fathers who abdicate their authority to their wives hurt future generations because their homes are not biblically aligned. This misalignment passes down to future generations as the sons of passive fathers become passive dads themselves while the daughters of passive fathers often marry passive husbands.

The Performance-Oriented Father

The last father type is the "performance-oriented" father. This father type misrepresents Father God by withholding love and affection when his children do not measure up to his standards of achievement. Performance-oriented fathers place tremendous pressure on their children to perform or be rejected. This downloads within them the lie: "If I am truly myself, I will not be accepted!"

Children who have been raised by performance-oriented fathers do not know how to rest because they are always striving to earn their father's approval and acceptance. They fear being rejected by their father and cope with this fear by doing "good works" to please him.

Psalm 103:4 tells us that our heavenly Father crowns us with lovingkindness (NKJV). He does this not because we have "done" something for Him but because He loves us as we are. Performance-oriented fathers, who give love and affirmation only when their children do well, paint an untruthful picture of God the Father to their kids. This often produces adult children who overwork, burnout, and become depressed. God the Father is looking for sons and daughters, not results!

God the Father is looking for sons and daughters, not results!

The orphan stronghold, once again, is a series of mind-sets impregnated with lies and vows that blind an individual from truly understanding who God is and from receiving His love the way He originally intended. These false beliefs and negative emotions produce individuals who do not know how to receive and give love!

In the next chapter, "Recognizing the Orphan Within Us!" I will share briefly how the Lord sent people into my life to help me see that I was functioning as an orphan.

Thoughts to Ponder

Chapter Three

1. The orphan stronghold is comprised of certain mind-sets or lies such as:

    - God doesn't love me!
    - I am not worthy to receive anything from God!
    - I don't belong in my family!
    - No one cares about me!
    - My feelings don't matter!
    - There is no such thing as a happy family!
    - The best way to avoid hurt is to isolate myself from others!
    - Significant people in my life will not be there for me when I need their help!
    - I am valuable to others only for what I can do for them!
    - Even when I give my best it is not good enough!

2. Vows are computer programs of the soul which when subconsciously made "protect" us from being hurt in the future. They are walls of protection erected around our hearts to keep anything or anyone from hurting us again. Some examples are:

    - I will never let anyone in authority tell me what to do!
    - I will never trust anyone in authority!
    - I will not allow anyone to get close to me because if I do they will reject me!
    - I will always be lonely!
    - I will always be on guard as to what I say to others or those words will be used against me!

Different Ways Fathers and Mothers Misrepresent God

Father-Mother Types[3]

Father-Mother Misrepresentations	Characteristics	Traumatic Events	Strongholds	View of God
Good (Perfect)	• Affectionate and expressive • Great provider • Affirming and present • Calls out destiny and purpose	• Premature death • Career ending accident • Unintentionally doesn't keep promises • Unintentionally hurts children	• Anger • Disappointment • Insecurity	• Angry at God • Doesn't believe God keeps His promises • Miscellaneous
Absent (Present)	• Father not home a lot • Workaholic • Nature of job or career • Divorce or separation	• Abandoned family • Misses important events like: - birthdays - sporting events - bed time - recitals, etc.	• Fear of abandonment • Fear of disappointment • Orphan mindset (left to figure out life on his own and therefore draws conclusions based on lies)	• God will not be here for me when I need Him most • I am unable to experience God's presence • God is not with me • God does not care about me
Abusive (Kind)	• Sexual • Verbal • Physical	• Incest • Constantly word cursed • Hit or punished • Abused mother • Adultery • Alcoholic	• Fear of punishment • I will never be good enough • Everything is my fault • I am responsible for my father's abuse • I will never trust authority figures • Hatred and unforgiveness • Loneliness • No one will protect me but me	• God cannot be trusted • God will not protect me • Feels distant from God

Father-Mother Misrepresentations	Characteristics	Traumatic Events	Strongholds	View of God
Authoritarian **(Loving)**	• Loves the law (rules) • Demands unquestioned obedience • Intimidates and controls via fear (also through tone of voice)	• Miscellaneous	• No emotional connection with father • Fear of father • No sense of destiny and purpose • Doesn't trust those in authority	• Sees God as a harsh authoritarian to be feared and obeyed rather than a loving Father to be enjoyed and cherished • Fears divine punishment • Feels like God's servant instead of God's son
Performance Oriented **(Gracious)**	• High performance standards expected of children • Gives love and affirmation only when kids measure up to expectations • Shame-based • Points out flaws in children more than praising their achievements	• Bad report card • Poor game • Didn't do chores well enough • Compared to others	• People pleaser • Strives for perfection • Fears rejection • Has a difficult time resting or slowing down • Gets burned out often • Feels down when they perceive they have failed God (self-rejection)	• God is not pleased with me unless I lead more people to Christ, read the Bible religiously and pray more • I must perform for God (instead of ministering from God) • God will reject me if I don't do enough for Him
Passive **(Active)**	• Not able to demonstrate love or affection • Does not share life experiences or feelings • Doesn't lead family (makes no great demands on his children) • Home but not home	• Father didn't speak to him much • Saw mother leading home and father in background • Has difficulty enjoying his family	• Home not aligned with the Word of God (wife leads home) • Has difficulty enjoying his family • Wife exhausted and/or burdened	• Relationship with God devoid of passion and joy • Intellectually connected to God—doesn't let God touch his heart • God loves me but only from afar

(The bolded words in parentheses reflect the perfect character qualities of God the Father.)

Small Group Discussion Questions

Chapter Three

1. Read John 5:43 and share with everyone what kind of parents you had (good; absent; abusive; authoritarian; passive; performance oriented).

2. Reread the list of lies (mind-sets) that orphans often believe listed at the beginning of this chapter. Do you believe any of these lies? Why?

3. Under the subtitle "Computer Programs of the Soul," Pastor Rob introduces the topic of vows. What is a vow and how can it hinder the way you relate to others?

4. Can you relate to any of the vows listed in this chapter? Can you recall any vows not listed that you made? Why did you make them?

5. Spend your remaining time repenting and renouncing any vows that have blocked you from trusting God and others.

Example: *In the name of Jesus, I repent of the lies that no one loves me and that I don't belong! I renounce the vow, Lord, that I will never trust anyone in authority. I bring these lies and this vow to death on Your cross and ask You to break its power off of my life! In Jesus' name. Amen.*

(Note: To *repent* means to have a complete change of attitude, while to *renounce* means to break legal ties with a negative or destructive attitude, relationship, or habit.)

Recognizing the Orphan Within Us!

4

When Jesus and his disciples were near the town of Caesarea Philippi, he asked them, "What do people say about the Son of Man?" The disciples answered, "Some people say you are John the Baptist or maybe Elijah or Jeremiah or some other prophet." Then Jesus asked them, "But who do you say I am?" Simon Peter spoke up, "You are the Messiah, the Son of the living God." Jesus told him: "Simon, son of Jonah, you are blessed! You didn't discover this on your own. It was shown [revealed] to you by my Father in heaven."
—MATTHEW 16:13–17, CEV

Panic in Colorado Springs!

In the late winter of 2002, I accompanied Pastor Cal Chinen to a Harvest Evangelism leadership summit in Colorado Springs, Colorado. After unpacking our bags and getting settled into our room, Cal and I made our way downstairs to check in at the conference registration table. As I stood in line behind Cal, I started to feel anxious and afraid, noticing that the conference was attended by high-level leaders—men of authority—from all over the United States.

When I got to the registration table, I was informed that my name was not listed for the evening dinner with other leaders. This not only intensified my level of anxiety but also triggered the feeling that I did not belong at the conference. To say that I was having an emotional crisis would be an understatement!

As I look back to this experience in Colorado Springs, I believe that the orphan structures within me were reacting to the "father" spirit that was strongly present in those attending the conference. That night when I called my wife in Hawaii she told me that she had had a dream in which the Lord had told her to tell me that I "belonged" at the conference. This comforted me, but I still felt like I had made the wrong decision to be there.

Clue

When I was a boy one of my favorite board games was Clue. In this game, a murder has taken place and the players have to figure out through various "clues" who the murderer is, the weapon used in the crime, and the room where it occured.

Individuals who function as orphans do not recognize that they are orphans. This is why orphans need "clues" to help them recognize and understand that they think and relate not as sons and daughters who are unconditionally loved by their Father in heaven but as orphans who have been conditionally loved by their parents.

The "clues" which reveal orphan structures of thought and attitude are traceable to the lies an individual believes and the way he relates to God, others, and himself. It is my prayer that the following orphan types "trigger" the revelation that you carry orphan structures within your soul.

> *The "clues" which reveal orphan structures of thought and attitude are traceable to the lies an individual believes and the way he relates to God, others and himself.*

Clue #1: The Lone Ranger

Feeling prompted by the Lord, I handed a young man a hundred dollar bill. I knew he was struggling financially and felt the Lord urging me to help him. Immediately he rejected my offer. When I asked him why he would not accept my help, he said he didn't know why. I realized at that moment that because this young man had had to face the world alone at the age of three because his dad had abandoned him, he had vowed never to acccpt anyone's help.

If you are a "Lone Ranger," your tendency is to function alone because trust was violated or destroyed at an early age. It is difficult for you to accept help from others because you were either rejected or abandoned by one of your parents. It is also possible that if your parents talked openly about getting a divorce or separation, your sense of security was shattered causing you to become fearful and afraid. As a result you concluded that anyone in authority could not be trusted.

If you are a "Lone Ranger," you feel lonely much of the time because you vowed not to trust others. Your fear of possibly being rejected or abandoned again is so deeply ingrained in your emotions that you believe functioning alone is the safest option for not getting hurt again. This "Lone Ranger" mind-set the Bible says is not only unhealthy but dangerous:

> Then they [the Danites] took what Micah had made, and his priest, and went on to Laish, against a peaceful and unsuspecting people.

They attacked them with the sword and burned down their city. **There was no one to rescue them** because they lived a long way from Sidon and had **no relationship with anyone else**.

—JUDGES 18:27–28

In the Book of Ecclesiastes 4:9–12, King Solomon emphatically states:

Two are better than one, because they have good return for their work: If one falls down, his friend can help him up. **But pity the man who falls and has no one to help him up!** Also, if two lie down together, they will keep warm. But how can one keep warm alone? Though one may be overpowered, two can defend themselves. A cord of three strands is not quickly broken."

Clearly, God does not want us to go through life alone (see Genesis 2:18) and grieves for us when we do.

Clue #2: The Mouse on a Wheel

If you are a "Mouse on a Wheel," you are probably a workaholic and find it difficult to rest or be still. Like the Energizer Bunny, you keep going and going! You live in performance mode all the time because you believe the lie: "I will be loved and affirmed only when I do well and live up to the expectations of others!" If this message was deposited into your heart and mind, you will be convinced that you must perform or work hard for God and find it difficult to enjoy life and others.

Many of us are familiar with the story of the Prodigal Son in Luke 15, but few of us have heard pastors teach about the older brother. Unlike his younger brother, who demanded his inheritance from his father and squandered it in a distant land on prostitutes, the older brother faithfully remained at home with his father.

Although the older brother was loyal to his father, he was loyal because he functioned from a performance orientated mind-set. He worked hard for his father, but he did so to "earn" his father's love. This is why he was so bitter and resentful when his father welcomed his lazy, no-good brother home and reinstated him into the family as a treasured son (see Luke 15:25–32).

If you are a "Mouse on a Wheel," God wants you to know that He loves you for who you are (His son or daughter) not for what you can do for Him. You don't have to earn His love, affection, and approval because you already have it!

Clue #3: The Faultfinder

If you are a "Faultfinder" you are quick to see the imperfections and faults of others, while being blind to your own weaknesses and misgivings. "Faultfind-ers" are typically raised by at least one "faultfinding" parent and are well acquaint-ed with what it means to be criticized. If you are a "Faultfinder," you probably see God not as a loving Father who unconditionally approves of you but as someone who is always critical of who you are and what you do.

The Pharisees were the religious leaders of Jesus' day. Well schooled in the Law of Moses (the first five books of the Old Testament) they were critical of those, who, in their eyes, did not uphold the Law. Not surprisingly, they were blind to their own sin (see John 8:1–11).

If you are a "Faultfinder," the Lord wants you to know that He uncondi-tionally loves you as you are. There is nothing you can say or do that will change His mind about you! Not only is He pleased with you, He likes you! Allow this truth to sink into your spirit right now, and ask God to give you the spiritual power you need to extend the same grace He gives you everyday to those around you.

Clue #4: The Doormat

If you are the "Doormat" type of orphan, you probably allow others to violate or take advantage of you. You may also struggle to maintain healthy re-lational boundaries because you were verbally, emotionally, or sexually abused during your childhood. Or, you may have watched your parents allow others to violate them, leading you to repeat their patterns. This abuse you may believe was your fault. If you are a "Doormat" type of orphan, the Lord wants you to main-tain healthy boundaries by not allowing others to take advantage of you. He also wants you to know that any abuses you suffered in your past were not your fault!

Clues #5 and 6: The Silent One and Controlling Wife

If you are a man who grew up in a home with a passive father and a con-trolling mother, you are probably a "Silent One." This means that you find it chal-lenging to express feelings to your loved ones and to those outside your family circle. You may also find it difficult to hear your heavenly Father's voice because your father rarely talked to you. If you are a woman who grew up in a misaligned home where your mother led your family because your father relinquished his authority, you likely deal with issues of "control."

Women often become controlling because they are forced to fill the lead-ership vacuum in their homes because their husbands are not doing so. Men do not lead their homes because their fathers did not lead theirs.

If you are a "Silent One," the Lord wants you to know that He is interested in "fathering" you. He wants to talk to you, spend time with you, and give you what you didn't receive during your childhood. He wants to encourage you to step into the role of leader in your home so your wife no longer has to bear the burden of leadership.

If you are a "Controlling Wife," the Lord wants to lift all the burdens you carry. He wants you to rest and trust Him. He wants you to know that "He" is in control. And, He wants you to allow (encourage) your husband to lead your home.

Clue #7: The Oblivious One

"The Oblivious" type of orphan is "oblivious" because he has no connection to his father and/or mother because they were "absent." This type of orphan is unaware of the parental wound in his heart because his "absent" father or mother did not do anything obvious to wound him during his childhood. His struggles are traceable to a lack of parenting and having to figure out how to do life on his own.

"Oblivious Ones" have a hard time seeing that their parental wounds have nothing to do with any painful incidents from their past but from the "absence" of what their parents didn't impart to them, had they been present, during their childhood.

Orphan vs. Sonship

There are other clues that indicate orphan structures of thought. The following chart from Shiloh Place will help you to identify orphan thinking comparing it to the thoughts of a son or daughter.

Orphan or Son[1]

THE SPIRIT OF AN ORPHAN		THE SPIRIT OF SONSHIP
See God as Master	IMAGE OF GOD	See God as a loving Father
Independent/Self—reliant	DEPENDENCY	Interdependent/Acknowledges Need
Live by the Love of Law	THEOLOGY	Live by the Law of Love
Insecure/Lack peace	SECURITY	Rest and Peace
Strive for the praise, approval, and acceptance of man.	NEED FOR APPROVAL	Totally accepted in God's love and justified by grace.
A need for personal achievement as you seek to impress God and others, or no motivation to serve at all.	MOTIVE FOR SERVICE	Service that is motivated by a deep gratitude for being unconditionally loved and accepted by God

THE SPIRIT OF AN ORPHAN		THE SPIRIT OF SONSHIP
Duty and earning God's favor or no motivation at all	MOTIVE BEHIND CHRISTIAN DISCIPLINES	Pleasure and delight
"Must" be holy to have God's favor, thus increasing a sense of shame and guilt	MOTIVE FOR PURITY	"Want to" be holy; do not want anything to hinder intimate relationship with God.
Self-rejection from comparing yourself to others.	SELF-IMAGE	Positive and affirmed because you know you have such value to God.
Seek comfort in counterfeit affections: addictions compulsions, escapism, busyness, hyper-religious activity.	SOURCE OF COMFORT	Seek times of quietness and solitude to rest in the Father's presence and love.
Competition, rivalry, and jealousy toward others' success and position.	PEER RELATIONSHIPS	Humility and unity as you value others and are able to rejoice in their blessings and success
Accusation and exposure in order to make yourself look good by making others look bad.	HANDLING OTHER'S FAULTS	Love covers as you seek to restore others in a spirit of love and gentleness.
See authority as a source of pain: distrustful toward them and lack a heart attitude of submission.	VIEW OF AUTHORITY	Respectful, honoring: you see them as ministers of God for good in your life.
Difficulty receiving admonition: you easily get your feelings hurt and close your spirit to discipline.	VIEW OF ADMONITION	See the receiving of admonition as a blessing and need in your life so that your faults and weaknesses are exposed and put to death.
Guarded and conditional; based upon others' performance as you seek to get your own needs met.	EXPRESSION OF LOVE	Open, patient, and affectionate as you lay your life and agendas down in order to meet the needs of others.
Conditional and Distant	SENSE OF GOD'S PRESENCE	Close and intimate
Bondage	CONDITION	Liberty
Feel like a Servant/Slave	POSITION	Feel like a Son/Daughter
Spiritual ambition: the earnest desire for some spiritual achievement and distinction and the willingness to strive for it; a desire to be seen and counted among the mature.	VISION	To daily experience the Father's unconditional love and acceptance and then be sent as a representative of His love to family and others.
Fight for what you can get!	FUTURE	Sonship releases your inheritance!

(Used by permission Shiloh Place Ministries.)

Depressed, Despondent, and Discouraged

Prior to going to Colorado Springs in 2002, a prophetically gifted man shared with me that in "2004 God would take me off the floor." Little did I know that I was about to plunge into a four-month long bout of depression and severe burn-out.

Being depressed for four months was difficult. I was despondent because I could not minister to anyone. God was healing my need to "do" to gain the love and approval of others.

Going Stir-Crazy

Unable to function as the senior pastor of the church I planted, I turned the church over to our associate pastor. During this time away from doing "good works," I slept, took walks, went to the beach, and learned to relax. Still, I was anxious because I thought I would be depressed for the rest of my life!

At this time a close friend of mine recommended that I go to a counseling center called Elijah House in Post Falls, Idaho. I filled out the necessary paper work and was scheduled to receive four days of counseling a month and a half later. The period of waiting was difficult, as I continued to battle extreme fatigue and restlessness—my Father in heaven was dealing with the unhealthy orphan structures in my soul.

You're Making Everyone Pay!

Before going up to Idaho, Barb and I were visited by our dear friend, Rod Washington. Rod's visit would prove to be pivotal as I began to get "cold feet" about going to Elijah House and expressed to him didn't need to get counseling. I was in denial! Good friends tell it like it is, and Rod was no exception. He told me, "You need to go to Elijah House because you are making everyone around you pay a heavy price!" "What do you mean?" I countered! In a loving tone Rod said, "You are making your entire family suffer because of the way you function and relate. You need to go to Idaho and get help!"

Stunned, I began to reflect upon what my dear friend had said to me. The words, "You're making everyone pay!" sunk deep into my heart. It was at this point that I realized I had been blinded to the reality that there were issues in my heart that were not only affecting me but also my wife and children. I needed help! Going to Elijah House was the next step God wanted me to take.

Barbara and I arrived in Post Falls, Idaho, in late April 2004. Although it was spring the land was still covered with snow. Psalm 51:7 says, "Wash me, and I shall be whiter than snow" (NKJV). I've always thought that snow is symbolic of

God's grace—His divine ability to "cleanse" and "cover" our sins. God was about to "cover" me with His grace over the next four days.

The Gondola of His Grace

The next morning I awoke from a dream. In this dream I was on a skateboard with one foot on the board and the other pushing myself up a hill. In the next scene I got into a gondola or cable car and was lifted to the top of a mountain. A few hours later, after meeting my counselor, I shared my dream with her. In an instant she said, "I know what your dream means!" Curious, I replied, "Would you please tell me?" She stated confidently, "God has brought you to Elijah House to take you off the mountain of performance [a skateboarder must power himself wherever he goes] to put you into the gondola of His grace. After you leave Elijah House, God is going to take you to new heights; but this time it won't be by your own strength but rather by the power of His grace!"

My counselor then shared a dream that she had that same morning for me about His plans for my life. I was stunned as she described the exact things God had declared to me about my future in a dream years earlier. Because of the depression I had given up on God's plans for my life, but my heavenly Father had not!

The next four days of counseling that followed can be described by one word—tears! I wept and wept as the Lord brought forth a well of emotions that I had buried deep inside of me. The release of these unexpressed emotions is how the Lord healed me of depression.

During one of my counseling sessions, my counselor asked several pointed questions in order to gain a clearer picture of my parents' parenting styles. My father, I told her, although very loving, never explained to me "why" he established and enforced the rules he did; and my mother, a Dr. Benjamin Spock trained parent, parented me very permissively.

My counselor explained that these different styles of parenting produced confusion within me and a lack of healthy boundaries. I was confused because my father never explained why I received the discipline I did, and I had no boundaries because my mom was so lenient. These different parenting styles caused me to feel insecure and led me to strive for the approval of others.

When my father died, as I shared earlier, matters grew worse because I lost my innocence and childhood and became "parentally inverted." With no husband to go to, my mom began to look to me for help. I went from being an insecure, confused, performance-oriented fifteen-year-old to a radically driven teenager who carried, like Atlas, the world on his shoulders. It was no wonder that I was a burned out, exhausted pastor in depression.

I left Post Falls a few days later with new lenses over the eyes of my heart. By God's grace, the orphan structures and mind-sets (lies) that had been steadily destroying my life and negatively affecting those around me had begun to lift. God, the amazing billiards player that He is, had positioned me for the next shot in my journey—sonship!

In chapter five, "My Father, My Father!" we will learn that God is a loving Father who wants us to "experientially" know that He loves us!

Thoughts to Ponder

Chapter Four

1. "Lone Rangers" believe that no one cares about them and will rarely accept help from God or others.

2. If you are a "Mouse on a Wheel," you do not know how to rest or sit still.

3. If you are a "Faultfinder," you are quick to see the imperfections and faults of others and yourself.

4. If you are the "Doormat" type of orphan, you were probably verbally, emotionally, or sexually abused by one or both of your parents.

5. If you are an individual who grew up in a home with a passive father and a controlling mother, you probably are a "Silent One."

6. If you are an "Oblivious One," you grew up with at least one parent who was also absent and received little or no instruction.

Small Group Discussion Questions

Chapter Four

1. What spoke to you as you read this chapter?

2. Pastor Rob refers to the "Lone Ranger," "The Mouse on a Wheel," "The Faultfinder," "The Doormat," "The Silent One," and "The Oblivious One" as names that describe the different ways orphans relate and function. Which one of these names can you relate to? Why?

3. Read John 6:63. What is the difference between "grace" and "works?"

4. What do you see God doing in your heart to ground you in the reality that you are God's "beloved" son or daughter?

5. Pray for each other as the Lord leads.

5

My Father! My Father!

As they were walking along and talking, suddenly a chariot of fire appeared, drawn by horses of fire. It drove between them, separating them, and Elijah was carried by a whirlwind into heaven. Elisha saw it and cried out, "My father! My father!"
—2 Kings 2:11–12, NLT

Covered by a Blanket of Security

In the late nineties I had the privilege and blessing of accompanying Apostle Sam Webb on several mission trips to Japan, Thailand, and Guam. On the trip to Guam, Sam and I were joined by others from the Grace Bible Church family from all over the world to celebrate the grand opening of New Life Covenant Church.

During this stay in Guam, I experienced church in a new and refreshing way! Prior to this experience, church for me was a Sunday event. But while in Guam I witnessed Sam and his wife, Nancy, pour into the Grace Bible family as parents would pour into their children.

On one occasion, Sam and Nancy took a group of us to see *Miss Congeniality*, starring Sandra Bullock. Another night they took everyone out to eat at Outback Steakhouse. And in between these special outings, Sam would connect with the men by taking them out for coffee while Nancy would take the women shopping.

Having grown up as an only child with orphan issues, being spiritually "parented" by Sam and Nancy along with their spiritual children was a wonderful experience! During this entire trip I felt like I was covered by a blanket of love and security! There was so much affirmation that I felt like I actually belonged to their family!

From Orphanage to Family

See, I will send you the prophet Elijah before that great and dreadful

58

day of the LORD comes. He will turn the **hearts** of the fathers to their children, and the **hearts** of the children to their fathers; or else I will come and strike the land with a curse.

—MALACHI 4:5–6

We are told in these last words of the Old Testament that before the Lord returns, He will restore the "hearts" of the fathers to their children and the "hearts" of the children to their fathers or the land in which we live, will be destroyed. From these verses it is easy to conclude that the restoration of the family is high on the end-time agenda of the Lord. On a worldwide scale, we could say that God is transitioning the church from a global orphanage into a global family. The point here is that God intends to restore one family at a time by healing the hurts and issues between fathers (and mothers) and their children. As this occurs families will be transformed across the globe!

In order for families to be healed, spiritual fathers will have to be restored to the Body of Christ. Like Elijah who "fathered" Elisha, spiritual fathers will be raised up by God to help the church transition from an orphanage to a family. These spiritual dads will live, model, and emphasize what I experienced while in Guam. They will see and relate to God's people not as attendees or members but as sons and daughters.

On a worldwide scale, we could say that God is transitioning the church from a global orphanage into a global family.

Spiritual fathers will also challenge and call forth men in God's household to rise up and lead their homes. They will no longer just provide for their families—they will lead them. This will have an incredible impact on their children and grand-children and will lead to societal transformation.

Why Fathers?

But the angel said to him: "Do not be afraid, Zechariah; your prayer has been heard. Your wife Elizabeth will bear you a son, and you are to give him the name John. He will be a joy and delight to you, and many will rejoice because of his birth, for he will be great in the sight of the Lord. He is never to take wine or other fermented drink, and he will be filled with the Holy Spirit even from birth. Many of the people of Israel will he bring back to the Lord their God. And he will go on before the Lord, in the spirit and power of Elijah, to turn the **hearts** of the fathers

to their children and the disobedient to the wisdom of the righteous—
to make ready a people prepared for the Lord."

—Luke 1:13–17

Like Malachi 4:5–6, Luke 1:13–17 tells us that the spirit of Elijah will supernaturally turn the "hearts" of the fathers back to the children. This begs the question, "Why the fathers?"

Before answering this question, it is important to understand that God has both male and female attributes (See Genesis 1:27), which He expresses through moms and dads simultaneously. One of God's names, "El Shaddai," reveals how God functions like a mother. El Shaddai or "God Almighty" is the Hebrew name for God, derived from the root word, "Shad," and is translated "breast." El Shaddai is the "All Sustaining One" who nurtures, comforts and tenderly cares for His children like a mother who nurses her newborn child.[1] Wow! God the Almighty comforts His children with the blessings of the breast (divine care, nurture, and sustenance)!

On the other hand, God functions as a father who "provides" for His family. In Genesis 22:14 God is referred to as Jehovah-Jireh, "the God who provides." A closer look at the root meaning of this word reveals that Jehovah-Jireh also means "the God who sees." God "sees" His children's needs and "provides"!

Let's explore briefly more about the mother-father aspects of God's nature by observing how the apostle Paul related to the family of God. Paul, the apostle, was much more than a church planter extraordinaire, an evangelist, a teacher, and a defender of the faith—he was a spiritual father who consistently represented the mother-father characteristics of God's nature to his spiritual children. In 1 Thessalonians 2 Paul wrote:

> As apostles of Christ we certainly had a right to make some demands of you, but we were **gentle** among you as a mother **feeding** and **caring** for her own children....And you know that we treated each of you as a father treats his own children. We **pleaded** with you, **encouraged** you, and **urged** you to live your lives in a way that God would consider worthy.
>
> —1 Thessalonians 2:7–6, 11–12, NLT

God created mothers and fathers differently in order to reveal the different aspects of His divine nature. When Paul related to his spiritual children as a mother would to her children, he was gentle, nurturing, and caring. But when Paul related to his spiritual children as a father, he pleaded, encouraged, and urged them to live wholeheartedly for God!

Let's return to the question: "Why the fathers?" Why does God turn the hearts of the fathers back to the children? By divine design, fathers have been chosen by God to be conduits of blessing to their children by releasing provision, protection, purpose, and peace (security). This is pictured in the Aaronic blessing in Numbers 6:24–26:

> May the LORD [your heavenly Father] **bless** you and **protect** you. May the LORD [your heavenly Father] **smile** on you and be gracious to you. May the LORD [your heavenly Father] show you his **favor** and give you **peace**.
>
> —NUMBERS 6:24–26, NLT

Jeff A. Benner, writing for the Ancient Hebrew Research Center, explains:

> The Hebrew word for "bless" is "barak" which literally means "to kneel." A berakah is a "blessing" but more literally, the bringing of a gift to another on bended "knee." When we bless God or others, we are in essence, bringing to them a gift on bended "knee." A true king is one who serves his people, one who will humble himself and come to his people on a bended knee.
>
> The Hebrew word for "keep" is "shamar" which literally means "to guard." A related word is "shamiyir" which means "thorn." When the shepherd was out in the wilderness with his flock, he would construct a corral of thorn bushes to protect the sheep from predators, a guarding over of the sheep.[2]

With Hebraic glasses we can now read the beginning of the Aaronic blessing as, "Yaweh will kneel before you presenting gifts and will guard you with a hedge of protection." The remaining portions of the Aaronic blessing can also be examined for its original Hebraic meaning revealing the following:

> Yaweh will knee before you presenting gifts and will guard you with a hedge of protection. Yaweh will illuminate the wholeness of his body toward you bringing order and he will beautify you. Yahweh will lift up his wholeness of being and look upon you and he will set in place all you need to be whole and complete.[3]

When fathers bless their children they prosper! But when fathers verbally abuse or curse their children they struggle! The word "blessing" also means to "add upon," while the word "curse" means to "subtract" or "take away." When dads fail to provide, protect, and bless their children, their children end up deficient in character, skill, and purpose.

Fathers are conduits of God's provision, protection, and purpose; but their calling is ultimately to introduce their families, wives, and children to "the Father." This means, dads, that you have been called by God to provide a clear, not perfect, snapshot of the Father to your children and call their spirit man to connect with the Spirit of God!

The Philippian Jailer

In Acts 16 a prison guard has an amazing encounter with God:

> The crowd joined in the attack against Paul and Silas, and the magistrates ordered them to be stripped and beaten with rods. After they had been severely flogged, they were thrown into prison, and the jailer was commanded to guard them carefully. When he received these orders, he put them in the inner cell and fastened their feet in the stocks. About midnight Paul and Silas were praying and singing hymns to God, and the other prisoners were listening to them. Suddenly there was such a violent earthquake that the foundations of the prison were shaken. At once all the prison doors flew open, and everyone's chains came loose. The jailer woke up, and when he saw the prison doors open, he drew his sword and was about to kill himself because he thought the prisoners had escaped. But Paul shouted, "Don't harm yourself! We are all here!" The jailer called for lights, rushed in and fell trembling before Paul and Silas. He then brought them out and asked, "Sirs, what must I do to be saved?" They replied, "Believe in the Lord Jesus, and you will be saved—you and your household." Then they spoke the word of the Lord to him and to all the others in his house. At that hour of the night the jailer took them and washed their wounds; then immediately he and all his household were baptized. The jailer brought them into his house and set a meal before them; he was filled with joy because he had come to believe in God—**he and his whole household**.
>
> —Acts 16:22–34

This passage shows that a father who has a relationship with the Lord Jesus opens the door for his entire family to trust in God also. (See also Acts 10:24–48, 11:14; Acts 18:7–8; 1 Corinthians 1:16, 16:15.) Scripture also shows us that mothers and single mothers can do the same (see John 4:1–42; Acts 16:15).

My Spiritual Fathers

As I look back to 1996, I now recognize how the Lord raised up Sam Webb to spiritually "father" me for a season. During this time I met with Sam regularly and traveled with him to Japan, Thailand, and Guam. I will always treasure the time God gave me with Sam because I experienced what I believe God's church is supposed to be—a family.

Later, God brought Cal Chinen, another spiritual father, into my life. Cal has been instrumental in releasing me into my calling through his counsel and spiritual oversight. The Lord also joined me to a third spiritual father, Dr. Paul L. Cox. Paul has been an amazing mentor as he has taught me how to exercise the spiritual gift of discernment but more importantly how to be a husband and father.

Fathers are conduits of blessing and introduce their families to God. Fathers also perpetuate generational blessings down the family line. In my book *Legacy of Blessing*, I shared how Abraham blessed Isaac who blessed Jacob causing each succeeding generation to begin their journey in God at a higher and more prosperous level. When a father understands the long-term impact of blessing his kids on a weekly basis, he impacts their future in a way that he cannot imagine. The same holds true for spiritual fathers who bless, affirm, and pour into their spiritual children on a regular basis.

Fathers Release Spiritual Inheritance

Whether you are a biological or spiritual father, God has called you to release your children into their destiny. In 2 Kings 2:12, Elisha cried, "My father, my father," as Elijah was snatched up by a whirlwind into heaven. Verse 13 tells us that Elisha then picked up off the ground his spiritual father's mantle (cloak). Elijah's mantle symbolized the power and authority God had given him to perform miracles for others. By leaving his mantle for his spiritual son, Elisha, Elijah released him to have a ministry far greater than his own.

The Bible records that Elijah performed fourteen miracles while his spiritual son, Elisha, performed twenty-eight. This "double" anointing was tangible evidence of the tremendous impact that a father or spiritual father can have when he releases his spiritual offspring into their inheritance. The present reality, however, is that few fathers know how to release their children into their inheritance because their fathers did not release them into theirs.

Stones and Obstacles

When fathers do not release to their children their inheritance, we must ask why? I believe the answer is found in two verses from the Book of Isaiah:

> It shall be said, "Build up, build up, prepare the way, remove every **obstruction** from my people's way."
> —Isaiah 57:14, esv

> Go through, go through the gates; prepare the way for the people; build up, build up the highway; clear it of **stones**; lift up a signal over the peoples.
> —Isaiah 62:10, esv

I believe God is saying in these verses that if we want to be prepared for global transformation and harvest we must allow the Holy Spirit to remove every stone and obstruction in our hearts that block us from knowing Him as Father. These obstructions (rejection, anger, abandonment, etc.) are generational in scope as fathers (and mothers) need to be healed of the hurts their parents inflicted upon them before they ask their sons and daughters to forgive them for doing the same.

Let the Fathers Arise!

As the generations are healed to one another, the church will be catapulted to a higher level of fruitfulness because fathers (and mothers), now free of their hurts, will be able to release their children into their inheritance. Revival will not only be sustained but will rise to new and powerful levels!

In chapter six we will discover how to "Break Free from the Orphan Stronghold."

Thoughts to Ponder

Chapter Five

1. On a worldwide scale, we could say God is transitioning the church from a global orphanage into a global family.

2. When fathers release the blessings upon their children that God wants them to release, their children will prosper!

3. The Hebrew word for "bless" is "*barak*," which literally means "to kneel." A *berakah* is a "blessing" but more literally, the bringing of a gift to another on bended "knee." When we bless God or others, we are, in essence, bringing a gift on bended knee.

4. The word "blessing" also means to "add upon," while the word "curse" means to "subtract" or "take away."

5. When dads fail to provide, protect, and bless their children, their children end up deficient in character, skill, and purpose.

6. Fathers are conduits of blessing and introduce their families to God.

Small Group Discussion Questions
Chapter Five

1. Describe your opinion of the ideal (not perfect) father.

2. How did your father pour into (and guide) your life? What has been the impact or lack of impact upon your life?

3. Read Malachi 4:5–6 and Luke 1:11–17. Based on these two passages, what is in your heart when you think about your dad—anger? thanksgiving? hurt? etc.?

4. What would you love to tell your dad (and mom) but have never been able to? What do you long for from your father (and mother)?

5. Pray for each other as the Spirit leads.

Breaking Free from the Orphan Stronghold

Jesus replied, "*I tell you the truth, everyone who sins is a slave to sin. Now a slave has no permanent place in the family, but a son belongs to it forever. So if the Son **sets you free**, you will be free indeed*."
—John 8:34–36

Every Orphan Has Core Pain

One morning I received an unexpected phone call from my friend Dean Fujishima. After exchanging small talk with him, he told me that he wanted to meet with me. Curious, I pressed him for more information; but he replied that it was better to meet with him face-to-face.

Later that day I met Dean and asked, "So, what's going on?" He looked at me and replied, "You're angry at your dad and God." I responded, "No, I'm not!" Dean repeated, "Rob, you're angry at your dad and God, and I need to pray for you!" Again I said, "No, I'm not; but if you want to pray for me go ahead." At that moment I thought, "No way! How can I be angry at God? I love the Lord! And, I loved my dad! There's no way I'm angry at either of them!"

Given the green light, Dean began to pray for me for half an hour with no results. Not one to easily give up, he said, "Rob, be honest with your feelings! Acknowledge that you're angry at your dad." Wanting to pacify Dean so I could go home, I did what he suggested, although with no emotion. "Dad, I'm angry at you." Dean quickly countered, "Rob, tell your dad how you really feel about him dying on you!" At that moment the Holy Spirit undergirded Dean's words and triggered a reservoir of angry emotions. To this day I am still in awe of how the Lord worked through Dean to release these emotions! For the next hour anger and hurt poured out of me like a waterfall as I cried over and over, "Dad, why did you leave me?"

Later, when I thought God was finished cleansing me, Dean said, "Rob,

68

there's more!" "More!" I uttered. "What else can there be?" "You're angry at the Lord because you believe that He took your dad from you!" "No, I'm not!" I blurted. "Rob," Dean said, "Tell the Lord that you're angry at Him." "I can't!" I said, "Rob, you have to tell Him!"

Like I did with my dad, I said with no emotion, "Lord, I'm angry at you." Dean persevered, "Rob, tell God what you really feel." "I can't Dean! How can I be angry at God?" "You are, Rob, now tell Him." To my great surprise once again angry emotions began to bubble forth and I began to scream, "God, why did you take my dad? Why God? Why?"

As I look back to that day in 1997, I can see that the Lord began the process of releasing me from the core pain that had taken root within me on September 14, 1974—the day my dad died; the day when I concluded that both my father and heavenly Father had abandoned me.

Steps to Breaking Free from the Orphan Stronghold

The first and most difficult step to breaking free from the orphan stronghold is "recognizing" that you are an orphan. Without this revelation you won't be able to break free from orphan thinking and relating. In his letter to the church at Ephesus, the apostle Paul gave us a key component for helping people recognize spiritual realities they have not been able to recognize: prayer!

The first step to breaking free from the orphan stronghold is to "recognize" that you are an orphan.

I pray also that the **eyes of your heart may be enlightened** in order that you may know the hope to which he has called you, the riches of his glorious inheritance in the saints, and his incomparably great power for us who believe.

—EPHESIANS 1:18–19

If you are the spouse or family member of someone who struggles with orphan structures of thought, attitude, and behavior, you must pray for them to "recognize" that they have orphan tendencies or they won't be willing to take the necessary steps to allow the Lord to transform them.

Humility Releases God's Life Changing Power!

If an orphan has loved ones praying for him to "recognize" that he is an orphan, God will give him the opportunity to see the light! Once he is able to recognize

69

that he has orphan mind-sets, he is ready to take step two, which is to ask for help. In 1 Peter 5:5–7 the Apostle Peter explains what unlocks the power of God on our behalf:

> All of you, clothe yourselves with humility toward one another because, "God opposes the proud but gives grace to the humble." **Humble yourselves** therefore, under God's mighty hand, that he may lift you up in due time. Cast all your anxiety on him because he cares for you.

To recognize that you are an orphan is not enough. You must also get help. Once I recognized that I needed help, I asked those close to me for their counsel and wisdom. Their feedback was what motivated me to seek counseling in Post Falls, Idaho, at Elijah House. For me to admit that I needed help and then getting that help was very humbling. Although difficult, I know that by taking this step God set in motion the process which eventually transformed me from an orphan into a son. He can do the same for you!

Extend Forgiveness to Your Parents

In Exodus 20:1–17 we find the "The Ten Commandments." In verse 12 God gives us the secret to having a long life, "**Honor** your father and your mother, so that you may live long in the land the LORD your God is giving you."

To honor means to "value," "give weight to," or "highly respect." According to God's word, when we honor our parents we will live long, prosperous lives. Conversely, when we "dishonor" our parents, our lives will not go well.

How Do We Dishonor Our Mother and Father?

When a parent "misrepresents" the Father to his child because of abuse, absenteeism, authoritarianism, passivity, or via performance expectancies, he wounds his child's heart.[1] Consequently, his child judges him for his imperfections and unfairness and negates the first commandment with a promise (see Ephesians 6:1–3).

Breaking free from the orphan stronghold requires that you first "recognize" that you are an orphan; second that you humble yourself by asking others for help, and third by purposely extending forgiveness to your parents for wounding you. This third step may be a tall order for you, but is nonetheless an important step for not only restoring God's blessings upon you but transforming you from orphan to son.

Take Responsibility for Your Sins

A fourth step for overcoming the orphan stronghold is to ask God to forgive you for your attitudes and actions toward your parents. Romans 3:23 states, "For all have sinned and fall short of the glory of God." This means that you must take personal responsibility for your sinful actions and attitudes towards your parents. When you do this you will begin to experience freedom and joy like you never have before!

> If we confess our sins, he is faithful and just and will forgive us our sins and **purify** us from all unrighteousness."
>
> —1 JOHN 1:9

Ask for Your Parents' Blessing

Although not possible for some, the most powerful step you can take when breaking free from the orphan stronghold is to seek your parents' blessing! Many people have not been blessed by their parents and, as a result, have not experienced the fullness of God's purpose and favor for their lives!

The ancient Hebraic practice of blessing was widely known and sought after in its day as the most important gift a father could bestow upon his children (see Genesis 48:20; 1 Chronicles 16:43; Hebrews 11:20–21). Receiving your father's blessing will release upon every area of your life a tangible impartation of God's favor. Don't delay! Go to your parents right now and ask them to lay their hands on you and release the blessing of God upon you. (For more information on how to bless your children, I recommend that you purchase Legacy of Blessing, available on Amazon.com.)

Spiritual Moms and Dads Can Bless You Too!

If, for whatever reason, you are unable to receive your parents' blessing seek the blessing of a spiritual mom or dad. Although not your parents, their blessing will be just as powerful and will catapult you to new heights in God and deepen your understanding of what it means to be God's son or daughter.

Repent For Being a Lone Ranger

One of the hardest steps for an orphan to take is to break free from the deeply ingrained pattern of doing life alone. Because of the lack of parenting, orphans have learned to do life by themselves. They believe, "If it's to be, it's up to me!" and often refuse the help of others.

Once an orphan has taken all the steps to break free from the mind-sets that have kept him from prospering, he needs to take one last step. This step involves repenting of being a soloist and purposely surrounding himself with others.

Persons who emerge from orphan relating need to deal with the lifestyle pattern of functioning on their own. In order for this to be practically walked out, they need to be slowly encouraged to share with others what they are going through. This is why they need family. A recovering orphan also needs to experience sonship. He needs to know that he can go to a mom or dad for feedback and help. He needs to know that he is accepted for who he is, not what he does. He needs to receive regular doses of love, which he did not receive while growing up. If an orphan has not repented of living life alone and believing that he doesn't need others, then he has not yet fully allowed God to transform him from orphan into a son.

Sample Father's Blessing Prayer

First, let me stand in for your parents and the authority figures in your life. There are words you need to hear that they may have never been able to say. Open your heart to forgive and release them as you hear these words.

My child, would you forgive me for my inability to show you true love? I wounded you in so many ways, causing you to turn your back on home and move away from love. Would you forgive me for each time I failed you? Forgive me for my high standards that left you feeling you could never please me. There were times when I allowed life to drain me so that I had nothing left to give you. Even when I was there, I wasn't there for you. Please forgive me for failing to show you the love in my heart.

Would you forgive me for my rules and requirements that left you no option but to rebel or to feel defeated and crushed? Please forgive me for pushing you into my mold rather than calling you to be who God made you to be and for all the pain that resulted. Please forgive me for leaving you without a safe place to call home and for turning my back on you and the family and abandoning you. God is not like that, and I misrepresented His love.

Please forgive me for the betrayal you experienced through my abuse—the words, the manipulation, the actions, the sins I committed against you. It was not your fault, and I ask your forgiveness for these ways that I lied to you about God.

Please forgive me for failing to show you tenderness in words or actions, for not holding you or singing over you. I ask your forgiveness for placing parenting responsibility on your young shoulders, taking away your childhood. My child, I am sorry for every way I failed you, hurt you, misrepresented God's love, and added to your pain. Please forgive me.

(Ask for a response; give comfort and unconditional love if appropriate)

Now I speak a Father's/Mother's blessing over you (Speak out each person's name if possible).

God has called you by your name, _____, and speaks your identity to you.

    Father God has chosen you to be His child, called by His name, adopted into His Kingdom to inherit all of His love in Jesus, our Savior and Lord. We welcome you as a member of His family and we bless you to know your identity in Him.

    Father God created you to know His love, to receive it, and to share it with others. We bless you to know this destiny in your heart and soul. You are called to live as a child of God, chosen and loved, forgiven and cleansed, released and set free.

    Father God speaks His blessing over you now and releases you into the authority and responsibility of womanhood or manhood.

    Are you willing to accept the promises and blessings of Almighty God and to do your best to walk in His ways?

(Ask for a response): *"Yes, I am with God's help."*

May the grace of our Lord Jesus Christ, and the love of God and the fellowship of the Holy Spirit be with you today and always. Amen.[2]

In chapter seven, "Rescuing Orphans from the Ungodly Depths," we will explore how to break free from ungodly places that parts of our soul are trapped in.

Thoughts to Ponder

Chapter Six

1. The first step to breaking free from the orphan stronghold is to "recognize" that you are an orphan.

2. To recognize that you are an orphan is not enough. You must also ask for help!

3. The ancient Hebraic practice of blessing was widely known and sought after in its day as the most important gift a father could bestow upon his children (see Genesis 48:20; 1 Chronicles 16:43; Hebrews 11:20–21).

4. Receiving your father's blessing will release upon every area of your life a tangible impartation of God's favor. Don't delay! Go to your parents and ask them to lay their hands on you and release the blessing of God upon you!

5. Once you have taken all the steps to break free from the mind-sets that have kept you from prospering, you need to take one last step. This step involves repenting of being a soloist and purposely surrounding yourself with others.

Small Group Discussion Questions

Chapter Six

1. Did God speak to any area of your life as you read this chapter?

2. Do any of you recognize orphan structures in the way you function or relate?

3. Do you find it easy or difficult to ask others for help? Why or why not?

4. How many of you have extended forgiveness to your parents for the way they hurt you? Why or why not?

5. Minister to one another as the Lord leads.

7 | Rescuing Orphans from the Ungodly Depths

*For great is Your mercy towards me, And You have delivered my soul from **the depths of Sheol**.*
—Psalm 86:13, NKJV

Was King David an Orphan?

As stated in chapter two, "Understanding the Orphan Stronghold," the word *orphanos* or "orphan" means "comfortless." When we understand the literal meaning of this word, we can conclude that at some level, whether significant or insignificant, every human being has been "orphaned."

King David was no exception. The youngest of eight brothers and two sisters (see 1 Samuel 17:12), David was the "forgotten" child. This scripture tells us that Jesse was "old and well advanced in years," indicating that he probably had little energy to parent his energetic young child.

First Samuel 16:6–11 tells how God sent the prophet Samuel to Bethlehem to anoint the next king of Israel. When he arrived at the city of bread, he asked David's father Jesse to gather his sons to "look them over." One by one Samuel looked with "prophetic eyes," hoping to identify the next king. After interviewing Jesse's sons, Samuel asked their father, "Are these all the sons you have?" "There is still the youngest," Jesse replied. "But he's out in the fields watching the sheep and the goats."

David, obviously, had been relegated to the fields to watch the family livestock. He was not qualified in his father's eyes to be *considered* yet alone *invited* to meet Samuel. Little did Jesse know that God had been training David to be a king in the sheepfolds! Like many parents, Jesse did not see his son's potential. This was not because Jesse did not "love" David but because he did not "know" David.

When parents (or a single parent) do not take the time to know their child, they will **not see their child's potential or be able to call it forth!**

I have met dozens of young men and women who have no idea who they are, what gifts and talents they have, or where they're headed because their parents were either absent or did not invest the time necessary to first identify and then draw out their potential. **Sadly, this lack of vision and foresight "orphans" children because they are left to figure out who they are in God and where they are headed by themselves.**

God sent a spiritual father named Samuel to call forth David's spirit to connect with God's Spirit and His plan for his life. Like Samuel, every father is called by God to speak to his child's spirit to encounter the Spirit of God!

The Devil's Schemes

In 2 Corinthians 2:10–11 Paul addresses the reality of spiritual warfare: "And when I forgive him (for whatever needs to be forgiven), I do so with Christ's authority for your benefit, so that Satan will not outsmart us. For we are very familiar with his **evil schemes**" (NLT).

If you have been a follower of Christ for any length of time, you are aware that **Satan is a master strategist.** John 10:10 reveals that, "The thief's purpose is to **steal and kill and destroy**" (NLT). So, how does Satan destroy families? And, what are his schemes, tactics, and plans for hindering your children's purpose and destiny?

What Are the Ungodly Depths?

One of Satan's primary tactics is to entrap parts of your child's soul (mind, will, and emotions) in what the Bible refers to as **the ungodly depths.**

To understand "the ungodly depths," let's turn our attention to Ephesians 6:12:

> For we [God's people] are not fighting against flesh-and-blood en-emies, but against evil rulers and authorities of the unseen world, against mighty powers in this dark world, and against evil spirits in **the heavenly places.**
>
> —EPHESIANS 6:12, NLT

According to this single verse, there are "**places**" of wickedness in the heavenly realms. The ungodly "depths" therefore is **a literal "place"** or spiritual "realm" in the heavens.

Names for the Depths

Throughout the Old and New Testaments there are synonyms that describe these

79

"places." Some of these are:

- Darkness (1 Samuel 2:9; Job 10:21–22; 12:25)
- Hades (Matthew 11:23; 16:18)
- Outer darkness (Matthew 8:12; 22:13; 25:30)
- Sheol (2 Samuel 22:6; Psalm 86:13; 116:3)
- The depths including "the ungodly depths" (Psalm 88:6; 107:26; 130:1)
- The grave (Job 7:9)
- The net (Psalm 140:5)
- The pit, including "the lowest pit," meaning that there are multiple levels in the ungodly depths (Proverbs 1:12; Isaiah 14:15; 38:18)
- The snare (Psalm 18:5; 91:3; 124:7)
- The trap (Psalm 69:22)
- Utter darkness (Job 10:22; 12:22)

How Does Satan Trap Individuals in the Ungodly Depths?

- When they experience extreme mourning or heartbreak (Genesis 37:35; 42:38; 44:29)!
- When they are in despair (Job 7:9; 14:1; 17:13)!
- When they worship idols (Deuteronomy 32:20–22)!
- When they commit murder (1 Kings 2:5–6)!
- When they are prideful (1 Samuel 2:3–6; Matthew 11:23)!
- When they rebel against authority (Numbers 16:1–30)!
- When they are sexually immoral (Proverbs 5:5; 7:1–27; 9:18)!
- When they are sick (Isaiah 38:10, 17–18)!
- When they are under tremendous stress (2 Samuel 22:6; Psalm 18:5; 116:3)!
- When they are verbally abused; gossip, slander, criticism, hurtful words spoken over others (Psalm 69:12–20; Proverbs 18:21)!
- When they themselves are slandered or criticized by others (Proverbs 18:21)!

Biblical Figures Trapped in the Ungodly Depths

1. David

I waited patiently for the LORD to help me, and he turned to me and

80

heard my cry. He lifted me out of **the pit** of despair.

—Psalm 40:1–2, nlt

But as for me, God will redeem my life. He will snatch me from the power of **the grave**.

—Psalm 49:15, nlt

For great is your love toward me; you have delivered me from **the depths** of the grave.

—Psalm 86:13

The **snares** of death encompassed me; the pangs of **Sheol** laid hold on me; I suffered distress and anguish.

—Psalm 116:3, esv

2. Jacob

And all his sons and daughters rose up to comfort him, but he refused to be comforted and said, "For I will go down to **Sheol** [the ungodly depths] to my son, mourning." Thus his father wept for him.

—Genesis 37:35, esv

Note: Jacob is feeling "**comfortless**." When an individual feels "**comfortless**," as many orphans do, they are stuck or trapped in the ungodly depths.

What Indicates that Part of You is Trapped in the Ungodly Depths?

- You feel brokenhearted and burdened!
- You feel conflicted!
- You feel disconnected, lonely, and abandoned!
- You feel fearful, stressed, and afraid!
- You feel oppressed!
- You feel tormented, tired, and troubled!
- You live in the present, but you feel like you are somewhere else!

How Do You Break Free from the Ungodly Depths?

If you struggle with the orphan structures and mind-sets outlined in chapter three, it is likely that part of you is trapped in the ungodly depths. To get out of the depths, pray the following prayer:

Prayer to Release One from the Ungodly Depths

Father, I repent and renounce for myself and my family line for all sins that have brought on the consequence of being entrapped in the ungodly depth, Sheol, the pit, the snare, and the trap, and have kept me bound and unable to fulfill my God-given purpose.

Father, have mercy on me, for I have endured much contempt and ridicule. Lord, break off the contempt and ridicule that has been put on me by the proud. Wash me from the arrogance and arrogant ways that brought the contempt upon me.

Lord, forgive me for not forgiving those who have come against me and entrapped me. I choose now to forgive those who have spoken contempt against me, and I release them to You.

I repent for all generational fear, especially the fear of man, and I repent for all those who ran from fear, thus causing them to fall into the pit.

I repent for all those in my generational line who caused conflict, strife, or disunity, especially in the Body of Christ.

I repent for myself and those in my generational line for pride, arrogance, deceit, anger, and fury. I repent for all generational adultery, harlotry, immorality, sexual perversion, ungodly bloodshed, and for all murdering of the innocent.

I repent for all those who had foolish lips and did not watch the words of their mouths.

I repent and renounce on behalf of myself and my family line for all who cursed father or mother.

Lord, I repent and renounce for myself and all those in my family line who did not walk in true spiritual unity but allowed bitterness, jealousy, and envy to be in our midst, causing us to fall into a trap and a snare.

Lord, on behalf of myself and my ancestors, I repent for all ungodly passivity that caused me to come into agreement with unjust accusations, ungodly perceptions, ungodly images, word curses, limitations, gossip, and slander that were sent against me or anything that belongs to me. Lord, please disconnect me from all these and cancel them. Lord, I now choose to come into agreement with Your perception of me.

Lord, please disconnect me from any ungodly physical touch, trauma, or assault that has trapped any part of me in ungodly depths.

Lord, please now rescue me and my family line from any and all places in the ungodly depth that trapped us, and restore us to Your True and Righteous depth and height—Your plumb line. Father, in Jesus' name, my desire is to be rightly related to You, to *have all that You intend to give me, and to receive everything that is in my inheritance. I ask You to open my eyes and correct my perceptions. Show me how to work out my salvation daily. Show me what to let go of and whom to extend forgiveness, so my position will change. Lord, I repent for self-righteousness and wrongly judging others. Lord, please remove the shackles, traps, and snares from my legs.*

Lord, remove me from the deep darkness of Sheol, the ungodly depth, fear, the snare, the trap, perdition, the pit, the darkest place, utter darkness, or the deep darkness. Lord, please remove me from the snares, traps, and nets that have bound my soul, my spirit, my body, and my health in the ungodly depths.

A Little Girl Breaks Free from the Depths

In the summer of 2011, I had the opportunity to pray for a "**comfortless**" ten-year-old girl whose father was in prison and whose mother had verbally and physically abused her. Before praying for this precious little girl, her grandmother, who had recently assumed legal custody of her, informed me that her granddaughter had bipolar symptoms and was causing disruption in her elementary school classroom.

In response I explained to her that I suspected her granddaughter was trapped in the ungodly depths. I shared from Proverbs 18:21, which states that harsh or abusive words can cause spiritual death or oppression when spoken by a parent over their child. Because her granddaughter had been repeatedly verbally abused, I explained it was likely that part of her granddaughter's emotions were trapped in the ungodly depths.

Once permission was granted I had the little girl pray the prayer enclosed in this chapter. Several days later I received a phone call from a person close to the situation who informed me that this little girl's behavior in the classroom had changed dramatically! Later, the grandmother reported that her granddaughter no longer had bipolar symptoms.

A Few Observations

It is my observation that children and adult children who are trapped in the ungodly depths are there for several reasons:

1. A lack of parenting or instruction: This causes a child to feel isolated and lonely, sending them to the depths.

2. Abandonment by one or both parents traps a child in the

ungodly depths because they feel rejected.

3. Cultural practices: A woman of Hawaiian ancestry explained that her husband gave their firstborn son to his mother to be raised. Her husband had been raised by his father's grand-mother and now it was his mother's turn to raise his son. Over three decades later the little boy who was taken from his parents to be raised by his paternal grandmother is in prison.

4. Family breakups: Whether divorce, the threat of divorce, or separation, family alienation causes tremendous upheaval and insecurity in a child's heart, sending them into the depths.

5. False religions: The Bible clearly states (see Deuteronomy 32:20–22) that idolatry will send individuals into the depths.

6. Punishment: Rebuke that is administered harshly without explanation can place a child in an ungodly place. Proverbs 18:21 tells us that the tongue can produce either life or death. When a parent speaks harshly to their child, they speak "death" over them, placing them in the pit of despair!

7. Traumatic incidents: Car accidents, getting lost, physical abuse, parental arguing, etc., can cause parts of a child's emotions to go into the depths.

There Is Hope!

If you think your child is trapped in a spiritual place that he can't seem to break free from (anguish, despair, hopelessness), he is probably in an ungodly place. Don't worry! Your child is just a prayer away from stepping into a new place of wholeness and freedom!

In chapter eight, "Receiving the Spirit of Adoption," I will explain how you can come into an intimate relationship with your heavenly Father.

Thoughts to Ponder

Chapter Seven

1. Every person, to some degree, is orphaned. This means that at some point during a person's childhood they longed to be "comforted," but for some reason were not. "Comfortlessness" stems from a parent not spending time with their child, speaking harshly to them, or physically abusing them, etc.

2. King David, a man after God's heart, was orphaned. The youngest of eight brothers and two sisters (see 1 Samuel 17:12), David was the "forgotten" child.

3. Like many parents today, Jesse did not see his son's potential. This was not because Jesse did not *love* David but because he did not *know* David!

4. When a parent does not spend time with his child, he will not be able to see his child's potential or be able to call it forth.

5. One of Satan's primary tactics for destroying families is to entrap parts of their children's emotions in the ungodly depths.

6. According to Ephesians 6:12 there are "places of wickedness" in the heavenly realms.

7. The ungodly depths are also referred to in the Bible as darkness, outer darkness, utter darkness, Hades, Sheol, the pit, the lowest pit, the net, the snare, the trap, etc.

8. King David and Jacob the Patriarch are biblical examples of people who were trapped in the ungodly depths.

Small Group Discussion Questions

Chapter Seven

1. Did your father encourage you to explore a wide variety of interests to help you discover how God created you? If not, how has the lack of self-discovery brought confusion to your overall understanding about your life purpose and call? If so, how has it positively impacted your understanding of how God wants you to live your life?

2. Can you recall an incident or season during your childhood when you felt "comfortless"? What happened?

3. Can you identify in any way with the ungodly depths? If so, how or why?

4. According to Pastor Rob, what indicates that part of you is trapped in the ungodly depths?

5. Pray together the prayer listed in this chapter to break free from the ungodly depths.

8

Receiving the Spirit of Adoption

*So you should not be like cowering, fearful slaves. You should behave instead like God's very own children, **adopted into His family**—calling him "Father, dear Father."*
—Romans 8:15, NLT

On a Plane to Israel

As I shared in chapter three, in February 2008 my son Jordan and I met a group of other fathers and their sons in Los Angeles to board a flight bound for Tel Aviv, Israel. The purpose of our trip was to explore the Holy Land together and bless Israel.

Once in the air I noticed an Orthodox Jewish father and his two sons seated near us. Throughout our fourteen-hour flight to Israel, I was deeply impressed with how this father cared for his sons. When it was time for his boys to sleep, he gave up his seat and stood at the rear of the plane so one son could lie flat across both seats and the other on the floor below. I was challenged by his act of self-sacrifice so his sons could get the rest they needed. But the one thing that touched my heart the most was when I heard his sons call him, "Abba," or, "Daddy."

The Baptism of the Holy Spirit

I listened intently as a pastor from Asia shared with me how his father spent time with his sister while he grew up but ignored him. At the age of fifteen he approached his father and asked him why he spoke only to his sister. His father replied that preferring girls was a family tradition. His father's answer devastated him! To make matters worse, his father died later that year.

For the next twenty-seven years this man's deepest regret was that he had never been "fathered." Then at the age of forty-two, the Spirit of God came upon him at a church gathering and he wept profusely for two hours while speaking in tongues and crying, "Abba! Father!" over and over.

Like this pastor, millions of believers have experienced the baptism of the Holy Spirit. When this supernatural experience occurs, a person's life is radically changed because they are encountered by the Father's unconditional love.

God Wants to Father You!

In 1 Chronicles 22 King David shared with his son and soon to be successor, Solomon, God's heart and plans for his future:

> Then David sent for his son Solomon and instructed him to build a temple for the LORD, the God of Israel. "I wanted to build a Temple to honor the name of the LORD my God," David told him. But the LORD said to me, 'You have killed many men in the great battles you have fought. And since you have shed so much blood before me, you will not be the one to build a Temple to honor my name. But you will have a son who will experience peace and rest. I will give him peace with his enemies in all the surrounding lands. His name will be Solomon [literally "beloved of the Lord"], and I will give peace and quiet to Israel during his reign. He is the one who will build a Temple to honor my name. **He will be my son, and I will be his Father**. And I will establish the throne of his kingdom forever.'"
>
> —1 CHRONICLES 22:6–10, NLT

Although God had great plans for Solomon, His greatest desire was to be his "Father." If you haven't received this revelation for your own life, put down this book right now and ask God to reveal to you what it means to be fathered. Tell the Lord that you desire to know and experience what it means to be His son or daughter.

It is my observation that although many in God's family know God as Jesus, they don't know Him as their "Father." Jesus said in John 14:6 that He is "the way" to the Father. Certainly most of us understand what Jesus accomplished for us on the cross at Calvary. Yet, many of us have yet to receive the revelation that Jesus went to the cross in order to bring us into intimate relationship with the Father. First Peter 3:18 states:

> Christ also suffered when he died for our sins once for all time. He never sinned, but he died for sinners that he might bring us safely **home** to God.
>
> —1 PETER 3:18, NLT

What's in a Home?

According to 1 Peter 3:18, home is where God is. Home is where your heavenly Father dwells. Home is a place of safety, security, affirmation, and most of all unconditional love. When you come home to the Father by receiving the Lord Jesus into your heart, God's Spirit takes up residence in you!

Your Heavenly Father is Waiting for You!

Many are familiar with the story of the Prodigal Son. In this Gospel account, Jesus paints a clear picture of God the Father as One who is waiting to forgive, restore, and receive wayward sons and daughters who have left the safety of His home and gone astray. Let's read the story in Luke 15:

> To illustrate the point further, Jesus told them this story: A man had two sons. The younger son told his father, "I want my share of your estate now before you die." So his father agreed to divide his wealth between his sons. A few days later his younger son packed all his belongings and moved to a distant land, and there he wasted all his money in wild living. About the time his money ran out, a great famine swept over the land, and he began to starve. He persuaded a local farmer to hire him, and the man sent him into his fields to feed the pigs. The young man became so hungry that even the pods he was feeding the pigs looked good to him. But no one gave him anything. When he finally came to his senses, he said to himself, at home even the hired servants have food enough to spare, and here I am dying of hunger! I will go home to my father and say, "Father, I have sinned against both heaven and you, and I am no longer worthy of being called your son. Please take me on as a hired servant." So he returned home to his father. And while he was still a long way off, his father saw him coming. Filled with love and compassion, he ran to his son, embraced him, and kissed him. His son said to him, "Father, I have sinned against both heaven and you, and I am no longer worthy of being called your son." But his father said to the servants, "Quick! Bring the finest robe in the house and put it on him. Get a ring for his finger and sandals for his feet. And kill the calf we have been fattening. We must celebrate with a feast, for this son of mine was dead and has now returned to life. He was lost, but now he is found." So the party began.
> —LUKE 15:11–24, NLT

If you have yet to experience the Father's love, He is waiting patiently for you to come home (see Luke 15:20)! And if you are a believer with orphan issues, know that God is the Father you've always longed for! Hosea 11:1 reveals that God viewed 1.5 million Israelite slaves as His corporate son:

> When Israel was a child, I loved him, and out of Egypt I called **My son**.

What was in God's heart when He freed the Israelites? His heart was to set them free from being a corporate orphan so they could become His corporate son (and daughter)!

Jesus Came to Reveal the Father

In John 10:30 Jesus said something so astounding that it rocked the religious world of His day: "The Father and I are one" (NLT). Jesus meant that He and God the Father were one and the same! Colossians 1:15 sums it up, "Christ is the visible image of the invisible God" (NLT).

God Wants to Adopt You into His Family!

Ephesians 1:5 says, "His [the Father's] unchanging plan has always been to **adopt** us into his own family by bringing us to himself through Jesus Christ. And this gave him pleasure" (NLT).

Years ago a family of ten from Maryland joined our congregation. The father and mother had eight adopted children from countries around the world and were about to adopt two more from the nation of Kazakhstan. Months later their new children, who had been living in an orphanage, were welcomed into their family. At the outset, their five-year-old son readily accepted his new mother and father but his fourteen-year-old sister did not. Although her reaction was expected by her adoptive parents, it still proved a painful season of adjustment for them.

I learned later that literal orphans find it extremely difficult to bond with their adoptive parents. The reasons for this are many, but the primary reason is that they don't trust their new parents. They find it difficult to believe that their new parents really love them and won't abandon them as their biological parents did.

In like manner, when an individual who has orphan issues receives Jesus as his personal Lord and Savior, he is brought to his new parent, God the Father, and his Father's family, the church. And like an adopted child, he needs ongoing "experiences" that the Father and His children are trustworthy.

Receiving the Spirit of Adoption

In order for a spiritual orphan to trust his heavenly Father, several things need to happen. First, a spiritual orphan must be healed to his earthly parents. This includes forgiving them for any offenses they committed against him and also taking personal responsibility for any unresolved bitterness or unforgiveness lodged in his heart towards them. Secondly, an orphan needs the ongoing affirmation of those in spiritual leadership (i.e., their small group leader, etc.). This will encourage him to trust those in authority since his experience of authority

91

has taught him otherwise. Thirdly, an orphan needs to have ongoing relationships with other members of God's family to counterbalance his tendency to do life on his own. And finally, a spiritual orphan needs to grasp the revelation that he has been adopted into God's family.

Have you embraced the revelation that God has adopted you into His family just as if you are His own son or daughter?

What is the spirit of adoption? The apostle Paul answered this question when he wrote in Romans 8:14–17:

> For all who are led by the Spirit of God are children of God. For you did not receive a spirit of slavery to fall back into fear, but you have received a **spirit of adoption**. When we cry, 'Abba! Father!' it is that very spirit bearing witness with our spirit that we are children of God, and if children, then heirs, heirs of God and joint heirs with Christ.
> —ROMANS 8:14–17, NRSV

Have you embraced the revelation that God has adopted you into His family just as if you are His own son or daughter? If you haven't, take a few minutes to think about this because if you are to overcome orphan thinking and relating you must embrace the spiritual and scriptural realities that you are God's child!

Jesus Gets Baptized

In Luke 3:21–22 Jesus is immersed first in water and then by the Spirit of God:

> When all the people were being baptized, Jesus was baptized too. And as he was praying, heaven was opened and the Holy Spirit descended on him in bodily form like a dove. And a voice came from heaven: "**You are my Son**, whom I love; with you I am well pleased."

Jesus was baptized, or immersed in water, and then in the Holy Spirit. What happened here? Jesus had an "experiential" encounter with the Father! He "felt" His Father's love and approval! Before Jesus began his three-year ministry at the age of thirty (Luke 3:23), His Father prepared Him by affirming Him as His Son! This is noteworthy because Jesus had not helped or miraculously healed a single person yet. We can conclude from this verse that God loves us for who we are not what we do!

If the Spirit of Christ lives within you, you are God's child in whom He (the Father) is well pleased! Take a moment right now and make the following declaration:

> *Father, in the name of Jesus and by the power of Your Spirit I declare that I am Your precious son/daughter! Holy Spirit, bear witness in my spirit that I am Your bambino and am a member of Your family forever! Come now, Lord, and tangibly touch me with Your presence! Amen.*

From Orphans to Sons and Daughters

As I stated earlier, the church is being transformed from a global orphanage into a global family. God sets the lonely into families (Psalm 68:6) not orphanages! Once we grasp this we will no longer function as church attendees but as sons and daughters. And as we are being transformed, we will impact our sphere of influence in the marketplace (government, the media, education, business, entertainment, etc.).

> For all creation is **waiting** eagerly for that future day when God will reveal who his children really are.
> —ROMANS 8:19, NLT

In chapter nine, "Divine Relating: The Key to Raising Healthy Children," we will look at several snapshots of how God the Father and God the Son relate to one another so we can learn to relate to our children in the same way.

Thoughts to Ponder

Chapter Eight

1. If you haven't experienced the Father's love and compassion, please know that He is waiting patiently for you to come home (see Luke 15:20).

2. If the Spirit of Christ lives within you, you are God's child in whom He (the Father) is well pleased!

3. God sets the lonely into families (Psalm 68:5–6) not into orphanages.

4. "For all creation is waiting eagerly for that future day when God will reveal who his children really are" (Romans 8:19).

Small Group Discussion Questions
Chapter Eight

1. Read 1 Chronicles 22:6–10.

2. Pastor Rob mentions in this chapter that God wants to "Father" you. What is your response to this statement?

3. Do you see the church as a place you go to or as a family you are a part of? Why or why not?

4. Do you know that you are God's child or do you feel more like an orphan? Why?

5. Have you embraced the revelation that you have been adopted into God's family as His son or daughter? If not, why not?

6. Pray for each other as the Spirit leads.

SECTION II
RAISING HEALTHY CHILDREN

Divine Relating: The Key to Raising Healthy Children

9

We did not follow cleverly invented stories when we told you about the power and coming of our Lord Jesus Christ, but we were eyewitnesses of his majesty. For he received honor and glory from God the Father when the voice came to him from the Majestic Glory, saying, "This is my Son, whom I love; with him I am well pleased."
—2 PETER 1:16–17

A Divine Encounter

In Matthew 17:1–5 we read of when Jesus took Peter, James, and John up Mount Tabor where He was transfigured before their eyes. Jesus' face shone like the sun and His clothes became white as light. After Jesus was transfigured into light, Moses and Elijah appeared and began to converse with Him.

As this Divine encounter on the mountain evolved, Peter offered to set up three tents for Jesus, Moses, and Elijah in which to stay. Matthew 17:5 tells us what happened next:

> While he was still speaking, a bright cloud enveloped them, and a voice from the cloud said, "This is my Son, whom I love; with him I am well pleased. Listen to him!"

As I have meditated on Peter's eyewitness account, I cannot help but wonder, "Why did the Lord Jesus want Peter, James, and John to witness what they saw and heard on the mountain?" I believe there is one primary reason: Jesus wanted these three men, whom He was pouring into as spiritual sons, to hear His Father speak to Him the words, "This is my Son, whom I love; with him I am well pleased."

Why did Jesus want these three "spiritual fathers in training" to hear His Father lovingly affirm Him? I believe the answer is found in 1 Corinthians 4:14–17:

> I am not writing this to shame you, but to warn you, as my dear children. Even though you have ten thousand guardians in Christ, you

do not have many **fathers**, for in Christ Jesus I became your **father** through the Gospel. Therefore I urge you to imitate me. For this reason I am sending to you Timothy, **my son** whom I love, who is faithful in the Lord. He will remind you of my way of life in Christ Jesus, which agrees with what I teach everywhere in every church.

Let's get back to Peter, James, and John. I believe Jesus strategically positioned these three "spiritual fathers in training" to hear how His Father "interacted" with Him. I believe that He purposely allowed them to hear His Father bless Him because He wanted them to have a firsthand experience of "divine relating." By allowing them to hear His Father bless Him, they would know how to "father" the many spiritual sons and daughters He would entrust to them after He ascended into heaven.

Vision and Knowledge

Proverbs 29:18 states, "Where there is **no vision** the people perish" (KJV), while Hosea 4:6 adds, "My people are destroyed for a **lack of knowledge**" (KJV). I have discovered that when it comes to parenting fathers have little vision or understanding of how God wants them to "relate" to their children.

In the New Testament the Lord makes fifty-nine commands regarding how He wants us to relate to one another.

Many have said that Christianity is a relationship not a religion. This means that God is "big" on relating! In the New Testament the Lord makes fifty-nine commands regarding how He wants us to relate to one another. Below are a few examples:

A new command I give you: **Love one another**. As I have loved you, so you must love one another. By this all men will know that you are my disciples, if you love one another.

—John 13:34–35

Carry each other's burdens, and in this way you will fulfill the law of Christ.

—Galatians 6:2

But **encourage one another** daily, as long as it called Today, so that none of you may be hardened by sin's deceitfulness.

—Hebrews 3:13

Be kind and compassionate to one another, forgiving each other, just as in Christ God forgave you.

—Ephesians 4:32

It is obvious that God wants us to relate to one another in ways that both glorify Him and bless each other! Your Father in heaven wants to teach you how to relate to your children by showing you how He relates to His Son. Think about this: the way you presently relate to your children today was not shaped by how the Father relates to His Son but by the way your parents related to you. To become a successful parent and son or daughter, you must trade your parents' ways of relating for your heavenly Father's way of relating.

Snapshots of Divine Relating

As a child I remember when my mother purchased a Polaroid camera. For those of you who know nothing but the digital age, this camera provided a clear snapshot (photo) in hand within a minute. In the Word of God we see "snapshots" of how the Father relates to His Son:

Snapshot 1: The Father is "pleased" with His Son!

> While he was still speaking, a bright cloud enveloped them, and a voice from the cloud said, "This is my Son, whom I love; with him I am well **pleased**. Listen to him!"
>
> —Matthew 17:5
>
> The Lord make his face [**smile**] shine upon you.
>
> —Numbers 6:25
>
> For the Lord **delights** in his people.
>
> —Psalm 149:4, nlt

Matthew 17:5 tells us that the Son is the "focus" of His Father's delight! It tells us that the Father loves the Son not for what He did or does but because He is His precious Son!

Parents, it is important to regularly express how pleased you are with your children just because! Your children need to know your smile and favor not only when they do something right but also when they do wrong!

Snapshot 2: The Father is always at His Son's side!

> The hour is coming, indeed it has come, when you will be scattered, each to his home, and you will leave me alone. Yet I am not alone, for **my Father is with me**.
>
> —John 16:32

102

I will **never leave** you nor forsake you.

—Hebrews 13:5, nkjv

Every son and daughter needs to know that his father will not abandon him or her to face the world and all of its pressures alone. Such was the case in John 16:32 as Jesus told His spiritual sons what was about to happen—they would abandon Him, but His Father would not!

Parents, your children need to know that you will never abandon them! If you abandon your kids, they will grow up believing that God will not be around to help them when they encounter various challenges! In effect, by leaving them you will deposit insecurity into their hearts causing them to face life tentatively at best.

Snapshot 3: The Father knows the Son intimately!

I am the good shepherd. I know my own sheep, and they know me, just as **my Father knows me** and I know the Father.

—John 10:14–15, nlt

In Hebrew the word *yadah* means "to know." *Yadah* literally speaks of the physical intimacy shared by a husband and wife. To be intimate is to be so connected to someone that you "know" them. In John 10:14–15 Jesus told His followers that His Father "knew" Him and He "knew" His Father.

Deuteronomy 6:4–9 is known as the *Shema*. In the Shema Jewish fathers are instructed by the Lord to disciple their children by spending time with them on a daily basis:

Hear, O Israel: The Lord our God, the Lord is one. Love the Lord your God with all your heart and with all your soul and with all your strength. These commandments that I give you today are to be upon your hearts. Impress them on your children. Talk about them when you sit **at home** and when you **walk along the road**, when you **lie down** and when you **get up**. Tie them as symbols on your hands and bind them on your foreheads. Write them on the doorframes of your houses and on your gates.

—Deuteronomy 6:4–9

Deuteronomy 6:7 tells us to talk about God's commands when we sit at home and when we walk along the road, when we lie down and when we get up. This command from the Lord was given to fathers, not mothers. Yet, it is the mothers who typically talk to their children. Dads, it is essential for you to talk to your children so they will experience what it means to have a relationship with you. This will prepare them to have a relationship with God the Father.

When Jesus walked the earth as the Son of God, He enjoyed a close relationship with His Father. Dads, enjoy your children! Pour into their lives by hanging out with them regularly. Ask God to show you what their gifts are and help cultivate them. Tell them what you think about them! Most of all share your hopes, your dreams, and yes, even your fears. This will pay tremendous dividends because they will connect with your heart—this is a major key to raising healthy, successful children!

Snapshot 4: God the Son did only what He saw His Father doing!

> Jesus said to them, "Very truly, I tell you, the Son can do nothing on his own, **but only what He sees the Father doing**; for whatever the Father does, the Son does likewise."
>
> —JOHN 5:19, NRSV

Dads, whether you realize it or not, your children are watching you! Years ago I was made humorously aware of this when I found a section of the *Honolulu Advertiser* on our bathroom floor in front of our toilet. This was strange until I figured out that my four-year-old son Jordan had repeatedly seen me read the newspaper while doing my morning business. I laughed as I realized that my little boy was copying exactly what he saw his daddy doing.

John 5:19 offers a profound snapshot of how the Son of God follows His Father's lead. Dads, your children are watching you. Whatever you do, they will do. If you pursue God, they will pursue God. If you read the Bible, they will read the Bible. If you relate to your wife in a loving way, they will do the same with their wives one day. If you serve God, they will serve God. John Sanford, the pioneer of inner healing, said, "A child does not become what a father says; he becomes what his father is."[1]

Snapshot 5: The Son consulted His Father for advice!

> But I do nothing without **consulting** the Father.
>
> —JOHN 5:30, NLT

In the Book of Proverbs chapters 3 and 4, each begin with a father exhorting his son to accept his counsel and instruction and live (prosper)!

> **My son, do not forget my teaching**, but keep my commands in your heart, **for they will prolong your life** many years and bring you prosperity.
>
> —PROVERBS 3:1–2

> **Listen, my sons, to a father's instruction; pay attention and gain understanding.** I give you sound learning, so do not forsake my teach-

ing. When I was a boy in my father's house, still tender, and an only child of my mother, he taught me and said, "Lay hold of my words with all your heart; **keep my commands and you will live**."

—PROVERBS 4:1–4

Jesus not only did what He saw His Father doing but He consulted His Father regularly for counsel. A prime example of this is found in John 8:1–11 when a woman caught in adultery was brought to Jesus by the Pharisees. Hoping to trap Him, they asked, "Teacher...this woman was caught in the very act of adultery. The law of Moses says to stone her. What do you say?" (vv. 5–6, NLT).

Verses 6–8 tell us that Jesus stooped down and wrote in the dust with His finger while the Pharisees waited for His answer. What was Jesus doing? Is it possible that Jesus was having an internal dialogue with His Father, wanting to know His Father's counsel? As soon as Jesus received His Father's guidance, He gave the Pharisees an answer, "All right, stone her. But let those who have never sinned throw the first stones!" (v. 7, NLT).

In 2009, I had an interesting dream where I was in the passenger seat of a Mini Cooper. Seated next to me in the driver's seat was a twenty-year-old man. As the dream unfolded, this young man was driving the car but I was doing the shifting—it was a standard transmission automobile. The Holy Spirit then spoke to me and said, "Rob, I want the rising generation and your generation to learn to work together to advance my Kingdom. You symbolize the fathers, while the young man symbolizes the sons. The rising generation will move quickly and powerfully like a Mini Cooper, but they will need your wisdom, counsel, and advice to get to the destination I have set before them!"

Many young people in God's family today are not fulfilling their destiny because they are moving independently of their fathers. Fathers, you are not supposed to control your children but empower them to be all that God has purposed them to be! Fathers, you are the bow and your children are the arrows. If you do your part, the rising generation will be shot into their destiny! And if the rising generation allows you to come alongside them, they will get to where God wants them to be a lot faster and with a lot less pain.

Snapshot 6: God the Father spoke gently and lovingly to His Son

Then a cloud appeared and enveloped them, and a voice came from the cloud: "**This is my Son, whom I love**. Listen to him!"

—MARK 9:7

Visualize for a moment the cloud of God's glory appearing and then enveloping Jesus, Moses, Elijah, James, John, and Peter on top of Mount Tabor.

And then imagine what God's voice sounded like when He said, "This is my Son, whom I love."

Many believers have asked me, "What does God's voice sound like?" The Bible says that God's voice is like a gentle whisper (1 Kings 19:12). God's voice is the voice of a loving Father. It is not harsh, authoritarian, angry, or frustrated. God's voice is full of tenderness, kindness, and compassion.

Dads, draw wisdom from this snapshot of divine relating because your tendency is probably to raise your voice and speak harshly to keep your children in line. My wife, Barbara, is a strong, secure, woman of God. Much of this she attributes to the gentle way her dad spoke to her as she was growing up, often calling her "sweetheart!" Our heavenly Father is the kindest person you will ever encounter! His voice will encourage and inspire you! His voice will affirm and validate you! His voice will make you feel safe and secure!

Closing Thoughts

Dads, call out to your heavenly Father to give you the supernatural power to relate to your children the way He relates to His Son. James 4:2 says, "You do not have, because you do not ask God," while 1 John 5:14 adds, "This is the confidence we have in approaching God: that if we ask anything according to his will, he hears us."

Dads, it is both the will and heart of God for you to learn how to relate to your children the way He relates to His Son. Ask, ask, ask! You won't be disappointed!

In chapter ten, "Different Ways Parents Unintentionally Wound Their Children," we will discover how parents unintentionally deposit insecurity, loneliness, mistrust, etc., into their children's hearts.

Thoughts to Ponder

Chapter Nine

1. The Lord Jesus invited Peter, James, and John to witness His transfiguration on the mountain, for one primary reason: Jesus wanted His three spiritual sons, whom He was pouring into, to hear His Father speak to Him the words, "This is my Son, whom I love; with Him I am well pleased."

2. Jesus strategically "positioned" James, John, and Peter, three spiritual fathers in the making, to hear how a father is supposed to relate to his son.

3. Snapshots of Divine Relating

   Snapshot 1: The Father is pleased with the Son (see Matthew 17:5)!

   Snapshot 2: The Father is always at His Son's side (see John 16:32)!

   Snapshot 3: The Father knows the Son intimately (see John 10:14–15)!

   Snapshot 4: God the Son did only what He saw His Father doing (see John 5:19)!

   Snapshot 5: The Son consulted His Father for advice (see John 5:30)!

   Snapshot 6: God the Father spoke gently and lovingly to His Son (see Mark 9:7)!

Small Group Discussion Questions

Chapter Nine

1. How did/does your father relate to you?

2. Read Matthew 17:1–5. Why did Jesus invite Peter, James, and John up the mountain?

3. Read Proverbs 29:18 and Hosea 4:6. What happens to us when we don't have vision for the future? If you are a parent, what are the possible consequences of not having vision for the way God wants you to relate to your children?

4. Review the six snapshots of Divine Relating listed in the "Thoughts to Ponder." Which one of these snapshots did God speak to you about your relationship with your children? Why?

5. Encourage each other as the Lord leads.

10 | Different Ways Parents Unintentionally Wound Their Children

*Fathers, **do not provoke** your children to anger by the way you treat them.*
—Ephesians 6:4, NLT

Parents Love Their Children

In all my years of counseling families, I have not met one parent who has intentionally or deliberately wounded their children. Many parents, however, without realizing the long-term consequences of their attitudes and actions, have unintentionally hurt their kids. This is the result of ignorance, lack of experience, and immaturity. How does this happen? Hosea 4:6 gives us the answer: "My people are destroyed for **lack of knowledge**" (NASB).

In all my years of counseling families I have not met one parent who has intentionally or deliberately wounded their children.

When we don't know God's blueprint (the Bible) for living our lives, life will not go well for us. So, what does God's Word have to say about the connection between a parent's actions and attitudes and the well-being of their children? It plainly states:

> I [God] lavish unfailing love to a thousand generations. I forgive iniquity, rebellion, and sin. But I do not excuse the guilty. I lay the **sins of the parents** upon their children and grandchildren; **the entire family is affected**—even children in the third and fourth generations.
> —Exodus 34:7, NLT

110

Parents are Gatekeepers

What is a gatekeeper? A quick glance at 2 Chronicles 23:19 reveals that during King David's reign Jehoiada the priest stationed gatekeepers at the gates of the Lord's house (the temple) to "keep out" those who were ceremonially unclean. In addition to guarding the entrance to the temple, the gatekeepers "protected" the city gates and had the authority to refuse or admit entrance to those wanting to enter the city (see 1 Chronicles 9:19–27).

The spiritual analogy here, moms and dads, is that you are called by God to protect your children from evil influences. To put it more bluntly, your actions and attitudes open the door for either good or evil to positively or negatively affect your children and your generational legacy!

Seven Common Mistakes

In Proverbs 6:16–19 King Solomon wrote:

> There are six things the LORD hates—no, **seven things** he detests: haughty eyes, a lying tongue, hands that kill the innocent, a heart that plots evil, feet that race to do wrong, a false witness who pours out lies, a person who sows discord in a family.
>
> —PROVERBS 6:16–19, NLT

It is my observation that parents unintentionally wound their children in at least seven ways. I do not base my observation on scientific research but on my own failures as a parent and my interactions with other parents and their children.

If you are a parent, my goal in writing this chapter is not to condemn you but to draw your attention to how you may have possibly wounded your children without realizing it. These seven common mistakes are:

1. Abandonment (or threat of abandonment)

In March 2011 a young man in my congregation told me that he felt that I had abandoned him. Although there was no basis for his claim, I realized that the Lord had worked through me to trigger a fear that was lodged in his heart.

Wanting to uncover "the root of his fear," I asked the young man's mother a few questions and learned that she and her husband had had marital issues when her son was a little boy. Heated words were exchanged, the word *divorce* came up, and her husband angrily declared his intent to leave. The boy heard everything and begged his dad not to leave as he left the house. Somehow I triggered this young man's fear of being abandoned and unintentionally hurt him.

Another youngster in his teens shared with me that when he was three years old his father packed up his belongings and left he and his mother for good. Several years later this young man flew into a violent rage towards me, perceiving that I had rejected him. Like the other young man, I had unintentionally triggered his core pain.

Parents, when you abandon or threaten to abandon your children for whatever reason, you sow into their hearts seeds of fear, rejection, insecurity, and anger. If not dealt with, these strongholds will manifest later creating a deep divide between you and your children. Unfortunately, the fear of being abandoned will also negatively influence the way they relate to others and the way they perceive God.

Like many couples, my mom and dad had their share of marital difficulties. When I was a little boy, my mother had an extramarital affair. Fortunately, my father forgave my mother and did not abandon us. Still, I grew up fearful, insecure, and afraid that others, especially authority figures, would abandon me. This caused me to relate to those in authority on a very surface level.

Parents, if you are talking openly about getting a divorce in front of your children or have already signed the divorce papers, your child's world will be ripped apart! In chapter eleven I will explain what you can do to help them overcome their loss of security.

2. In Utero Wounds

A second mistake parents unintentionally make is exposing their unborn children to their hurts during pregnancy. Of course, the vast majority of parents aren't aware of how their child can be emotionally and spiritually wounded during pregnancy.

An unborn child is obviously connected primarily to his mother during pregnancy. This means that whatever a mother is experiencing physically, emotionally, and spiritually can and is imparted to her unborn child. It also means that an individual's primary wound can be traced to his mother. Not only is a child exposed to his mother's emotions during pregnancy but also during the first year if she nurses him. In the chart below by John and Paula Stanford are clues that identify several ways that a mother (and father) unknowingly hurt their unborn child:

Clues for Identification of In Utero Wounds[1]

The condition in utero	Commonly observed patterns of attitude and behavior after birth
Child is not wanted	Striving, performance oriented, tries to earn the right to be, shows an inordinate desire to please (or the opposite, rejects others before he can be rejected), tense, apologetic, angry, wants to die, frequently ill, cannot bond, refuses affection (or has an insatiable desire for affection)
Child is conceived out of wedlock	Has a deep sense of shame, lack of belonging
Parents face a bad time financially	Believes, "I'm a burden."
Parents are too young, not ready	Believes, "I'm an intrusion."
Mother has poor health	Feeling guilty for being; may take emotional responsibilities for mother
Child being formed is what one or both parents consider to be the wrong sex	Sexual identification problems, sometimes one of the causes of homosexuality, strives to please to be what the parents want, has a defeatist attitude, "I was wrong from the beginning."
This child follows other conceptions that were lost	Over-serious, over-achieving, strives, tries to make up for the loss, angry at being a "replacement" etc.
Mother has inordinate fear of delivery	Fearful, insecure, fear of childbirth
Fighting in the home	Nervousness, uptightness, fear, jumpiness, jumping in to control a discussion when differences of opinion emerge, feeling guilty: "I'm the reason for the quarrel," parental inversion: taking emotional responsibility for the parents
Father dies or leaves	Feels guilty, blames self, anger, bitter-root expectation, may have a death wish, depressed
Mother loses a loved one and is consumed by grief	Sadness, depressed, has a death wish, fears death, loneliness, imagines "no support for me; I will have to depend on myself."
Unwholesome sexual relations, father's approaches to mother are insensitive or violent—or more than one sexual partner	Aversion to sex, fears male organ, general unhealthy attitude
Mother is afraid of gaining too much weight, does not eat properly	Insatiable hunger, angry
Mother a heavy smoker	Predisposition to severe anxiety
Mother consumes too much caffeine	Baby likely to have poor muscle tone and low activity level
Mother consumes alcohol	More than the chemical effect, the baby absorbs the negative feelings which caused the mother to drink. Breech delivery, higher risk of having learning problems
Unusually painful delivery	Angry, has ulcers, depressed

Relatively normal delivery	Fury if pain, mother's or child's, seems to confirm rejection or ambivalence in utero
Induced labor	Can affect mother-child bonding, masochistic personality or sexual perversion
C-section	Intense craving for all kinds of physical contact, has trouble with concept of space, clumsy
Cord around neck	Throat-related problems, swallowing, speech impediments, anti-social or criminal behavior

(Table taken from Healing the Wounded Spirit by John and Paula Stanford.)

3. Lack of Involvement

The third way parents unintentionally hurt their children is by not taking the time to be involved with their interests and challenges. The reasons for a parent's lack of involvement may range from being focused more on building their career than building their family to simply not knowing how to relationally connect with their kids.

Parental non-involvement can take several forms such as:

a. Not talking to your children.

As I already mentioned in chapter eight, I listened to a man tell me that the greatest regret of his life was not knowing his father. If you recall, his father spoke to his sister but not to him.

b. Not teaching your children the "basics" of life.

A key leader in a large church on Oahu told me during a counseling session that he felt like he could never reach his potential as an adult. He expressed how angry he was at his father for not only abandoning him but for never teaching him the basics of life like how to drive a car. He was angry at his dad because he had to figure out everything on his own.

c. Not spending time with your children.

Two months before his death, Apple co-founder, Steve Jobs, introduced his children to the man who was writing his life biography. Apparently, Jobs wanted his children to know why he wasn't there for them while they were growing up. Sadly, the man who had impacted the computer industry, the phone industry, the movie industry, and the music industry had failed to impact his children because he was working twenty hours a day.

d. Not expressing empathy or understanding when appropriate. Because of cultural and generational differences, parents are sometimes not able to understand what their children are going through. During her mid-twenties my mom returned home from a horrific experience on a New York freeway. While on the freeway her windshield wipers had failed during a rainstorm. Upon her return home she told her mom what happened. Instead of being empathetic, my grandmother scolded my mom for being overly emotional and making a big deal out of nothing. This deeply wounded my mother and negatively affected her relationship with her mom.

e. Not being physically affectionate

In Asian families love is commonly expressed by "doing things" for family members. This includes helpful acts of service and purchasing nice gifts. Although many families express their love by doing things for one another, they don't know how to express themselves through physical affection (hugs and kisses). This lack of physical touch within the family, I believe, wounds children because it creates an inability to give and receive love.

f. Not blessing their children but instead being constantly critical of them.

Often I will ask those attending workshops I give on the topic of blessing if they were verbally blessed by their parents while growing up. The result is always the same: few if any raise their hands. But, when I ask how many were criticized, ridiculed, or put down by their parents, almost every hand goes up.

Parents, your words carry the power to build up or tear down your children's self-esteem. For every word of correction, your kids need ten words of affirmation. If you don't do this, your children will grow up lacking confidence and self-esteem.

g. Mental illness

A woman in the congregation I pastor shared that she was raised by her older sisters because her mother was mentally ill. Her mother became mentally ill after her eighteen-month-old son died. This woman had no idea how her mother's absence, because of mental illness, had affected her life! Because she had been raised by her older sisters, she is the ninth of eleven children, she had not experienced her mother's care or nurture. Later, when she had her own children, she didn't realize that she did not nurture them. Why? She had not been "mothered" by her mother.

4. Parental Inversion

Parental inversion occurs when a child relinquishes his childhood and begins to function like a parent because his mother or father has died, abandoned the family, left home because of divorce, or is simply not functioning responsibly as a parent should. Normally, the "only" or "oldest" child is the one who steps into the role of parent. As a result, he (or she) loses his childlikeness (spontaneity, etc.) and concludes that if he doesn't take care of his family the family will fall apart.

Parentally inverted individuals often become both "workaholics," who do not know how to rest, and "burden bearers" who believe they are responsible for everyone. They tend to be perfectionists.

A man in his twenties told me that after his mom and dad got divorced he stepped into the role of father and began to help his mom parent his younger sisters. This eventually became an unbearable burden for him because his sisters expected him to provide for their financial needs and solve their problems.

5. Quarreling

Another mistake parents commonly make that hurts their children is quarreling. While on a mission trip to Ireland, a man informed me that his daughter had asthma and wanted to receive prayer. I responded by asking him if he and his wife argued a lot when their daughter was a child. He promptly said that they had not.

A week later I met with the daughter and asked her if her parents quarreled frequently when she was a child. Her quick reply was, "Yes!" She then recalled a vivid memory of her huddling together with her younger twin brothers in their bedroom in an effort to shield them from the ugly exchange taking place in their parents' room nearby. At this point it became apparent that this woman's asthma was rooted in her childhood fear that her parents would abandon her and her younger brothers. Once she forgave her parents for arguing and renounced her fears, the Lord released healing into her lungs! Her father reported several weeks later via an e-mail that she was breathing much better!

In Exodus 17:1–13 we read of how the Israelites, at the Lord's command, camped at a place called Rephidim. When the 1.5 million-member Israelite community realized that there was no water for them to drink, they began to quarrel with Moses. Moses then sought the Lord, and the Lord instructed him to strike "the rock" on Mount Sinai. Out of obedience Moses struck the rock and water came gushing out.

This passage reveals a spiritual principal that I believe is a serious warning for parents who quarrel in front of their children. Verse 8 says:

> While the people of Israel were still at Rephidim [where they had just argued with Moses] **the warriors of Amalek attacked them**.
> —Exodus 17:8, nlt

This is the principle: Internal conflict or quarreling leads to an external oppressor (demonic attack). Let's frame this another way. Quarreling opens the door for the devil to attack your children! Bitter contention between you and your spouse gives Satan the legal right to infiltrate your home and steal your children's peace and security. Once this has occurred, your children will fear that you will abandon them and they may begin to have asthma.

A teenager told me that the darkest season of his life occurred while his parents argued regularly. During this time he said that it felt like his world began to crumble, and not surprisingly, he said he contracted asthma. It's time for all of us to heed what Proverbs 18:21 says: "**The tongue can bring death or life**; those who love to talk (argue) will reap the consequences" (nlt).

6. Sexual Impurity

At the beginning of this chapter, I defined what a gatekeeper is and explored its correlation to parents and their children. The point I was trying to make was that parents pass the effects of their sins to their children. This is certainly the case when it comes to sexual impurity.

It is obvious today, as it has been for centuries, that the devil systematically attempts to slime society with a river filled with sexual impurity. Whether through the movie industry, television, cell phones (sexting), or the internet, the devil bombards families with sexually charged messages designed to evoke immoral behavior.

When the Israelites traveled to the plains of Moab, Balak their king hired

Balaam son of Beor to curse them (see Numbers 22:1–6). Balak's plan backfired, however, when Balaam blessed the Israelites three times (24:10)!

Although the Israelites were not hindered by Balak's attempt to have them cursed, they fell prey shortly thereafter to sexual temptation. Numbers 25:1 says:

> While the Israelites were camped at Acacia Grove, some of the men **defiled themselves** by having sexual relations with local Moabite women.
> —NUMBERS 25:1, NLT

Parents, one of the devil's primary schemes against your family is to first defile you sexually so you pass the defilement on to your children. King David, Israel's greatest king, fell into sexual temptation by committing adultery with Bathsheba (see 2 Samuel 11:2–4). Little did David realize how that single moment of illicit passion would negatively impact not only his son Solomon, but the entire nation of Israel itself (see 1 Kings 11:1–13)!

7. Unrealistic Expectations

I sat with a man gazing across Waikiki beach out towards the Pacific Ocean. After exchanging small talk, he opened up to me and recounted how his father expected him to be a goal setting, high achievement, individual like himself. He shared that for his entire life he lived in fear of not being able to meet his father's expectations. By the end of our conversation, he realized that he was angry with his father because his father had not recognized that he was a creatively wired person (a musician) not a businessman.

Part of a parent's job description is to help their child discover their unique gifts, talents, and temperament so they can become the person God intended them to become instead of the person they want them to be. If a parent is bent on his child becoming who he wants him to be, he will instill the fear of rejection and the fear of failure in his child's heart. But, if a parent asks the Lord to give him "eyes" to see how He has created his child, he can develop and draw out those God-given gifts and talents accordingly.

In chapter eleven, "Reconciling with Your Children Begins with an Apology," you will learn that humility is the key to restoring broken relationships.

Thoughts to Ponder

Chapter Ten

1. The majority of parents do not intentionally or deliberately wound their children. Many parents, however, without realizing the long-term consequences of their attitudes and actions, have unintentionally hurt their kids. This is the result of ignorance, lack of experience, and immaturity.

2. Read Exodus 34:7.

3. Parents, you have been called by God to protect your children from evil influences. God has tied every generation to past and succeeding generations. This means that the consequences of your sins (unrighteous actions and attitudes) will pass to your children.

4. Parents unintentionally wound their children in at least seven ways:
    - Through abandonment (or threat of abandonment)
    - Through in utero wounds
    - Through lack of involvement
    - Through parental inversion
    - Through quarreling
    - Through sexual impurity
    - Through unrealistic expectations

Small Group Discussion Questions

Chapter Ten

1. What positive attitudes, traits, characteristics, habits, etc., did your father pass to you that you can be thankful for? Your mother?

2. In this chapter Pastor Rob lists seven common mistakes that parents make that unintentionally wound their children. As a parent, have you made at least one of these mistakes? If so, how? And, can you recognize how this affected your child(ren)?

3. Now that you have acknowledged that you have wounded your children, are you willing to go to them and apologize for what you did? Further, are you willing to allow them to share (give you feedback) with you how they felt when you wounded them?

4. Encourage and pray for one another as the Lord leads.

11

Reconciling with Your Children Begins with an Apology

*Therefore **confess your sins** to each other and pray for each other so that you may be healed.*
—JAMES 5:16

A Heartfelt Apology

As I prepared a message about parenting for the Kingdom Families Hawaii conference in November 2009, I heard the Holy Spirit whisper, "Rob, before you speak I want you to kneel before your son Jordan and tell him that you are sorry for years of authoritarian parenting."

In response to what I heard the Lord say to me, I invited my son Jordan to attend the night I was scheduled to speak. In my heart I knew that the Lord was about to heal my son and me!

As I stood before the conference attendees, I explained what I was about to do and why. I then kneeled before Jordan, looked him in the eyes, and apologized for all the times I had gotten angry at him and wounded his heart. Instantly, my twenty-five-year-old son burst into tears. It was a "God" moment for both of us! God had turned my "heart" toward my son and vice versa.

Breakthroughs at Home

Four years earlier in 2005 my second son, Brandon, let me know very clearly that he did not want me to attend his baseball practices. At this time he was a member of the Junior Varsity baseball team for Castle High School. For some reason my presence bothered him, so I did my best to honor his wishes and stayed away from the baseball diamond.

Later, the Lord revealed why Brandon was so angry. Soon after he was born, he began to have difficulty breathing. Because of this he was placed in an incubator for a week of observation. The Lord showed me that during this period

122

of separation, my wife and I had unintentionally opened the door for the spirit of abandonment to attach itself to Brandon's soul.

One evening after Brandon came home from baseball practice, I told him that his mother and I wanted to speak to him. I shared with Brandon what God had showed us and we apologized to him for leaving him in the hospital all by himself. Tears gushed from his eyes and ours. God had healed our son of a deep wound! My son embraced me that night and our relationship was restored. And yes, he invited me back to the baseball diamond!

Recently, our family celebrated our weekly Sabbath meal and our third son's twentieth birthday. In Jewish culture the twelfth and twentieth years are significant. The twelfth year is the year a Jewish boy assumes responsibilities for his own actions before God during a ceremony called Bar Mitzvah—*bar* means son and *mitzvah* means commandments (see Luke 2:42). The twentieth year is the year a Jewish man is considered ready to go to war (see Numbers 1:1–3).

After I finished blessing my two older sons, Jordan and Brandon, I told everyone that I wanted to bless Jonathan in a special way. One by one, starting with Jon's older brothers and then my wife, we each shared words of encouragement with him. Jon was visibly touched by our heartfelt expressions of love for him!

My wife, Barbara, had told me previously that she could tell that Jon did not feel like he was a part of our family. She said that he felt this way because I had not poured into him as much as I had with Jordan and Brandon. Ouch!

When it came time for me to share with Jon I remembered my wife's insights and asked Jon to forgive me for not spending time with him like I had with his brothers. I tearfully apologized to Jon for dedicating most of my time to the church I had planted instead of him (Jon was born right before my wife and I planted Mountain View Community Church).

Jon wept as I repented for not carrying him in my heart during his early years. Today, Jon feels like a part of our family and, even better, our relationship as father and son has never been better!

The Power of Confession

James 5:16 says, "**Confess your sins** to each other and pray for each other so that you may be healed."

In the Greek language the word translated *confess* literally means "to agree with." When we confess our sins to one another and to God, we are not making God aware of our sin but are agreeing with Him that we have done wrong. James 5:16 tells us that divine healing follows personal confession, while 1 John 1:9

explains that confession leads to cleansing:

> If we confess our sins, he is faithful and just and will forgive us our sins and **purify** us from all unrighteousness.

A Mother's Confession

In the summer of 2011 I had a dream about a young man in our congregation. In the dream he was very angry with his mother. I awoke and wondered, "What is this about?"

Several days later I called the young man's mother and shared what the Lord had shown me. Hesitantly, she recounted how she had had an affair while pregnant with her son. She also shared that she was terribly afraid to tell him about the affair for fear that he would reject her—her son had exploded in anger at her many times!

I explained to this dear woman that she had allowed the spirit of jealousy to "hook" her son. This occurred, I continued, when she had had the affair.

The spirit of jealousy is a spiritual entity that "displaces" an individual from a position of favor. When this woman had had the affair, she invited this spirit to displace her husband. Her son, who was growing in her womb, was "hooked" by this spirit and regularly dealt with "jealousy" in his life.

After many months of grappling with the gentle nudging of the Lord, this woman found the courage to sit down with her son and confess what happened. At first he was angry and did not speak to her for weeks, but eventually forgave her!

Don't Let Your Pride Get in the Way!

King Solomon stated something every parent needs to know:

> **Pride** goes before destruction, and haughtiness before a fall.
> —PROVERBS 16:18, NLT

Peter echoed the same sentiment:

> God sets himself against **the proud,** but he shows favor to the humble.
> —1 PETER 5:5, NLT

What is God saying to us through King Solomon and Peter? He is saying pride keeps us from receiving His help but humility releases His assistance. It takes humility to apologize to someone we have injured and courage to say, "I'm sorry. I was wrong. Please forgive me."

It takes humility to apologize to someone that we have injured.

Parents, don't let pride get in the way of apologizing to your children. Don't expect them to make the first move. You are the adults. Initiate the apology and watch God move! Proverbs 28:13 says:

> People who cover their sins will not prosper. But if they confess and forsake them, **they will receive mercy**.
>
> —Proverbs 28:13, NLT

Recognizing the Need to Apologize and Reconcile with Your Children

I have observed that in addition to pride, many parents do not apologize for the hurts they have inflicted upon their children simply because they do not recognize that they have hurt them. If you are reading this chapter and are longing for your father or mother to apologize to you for the ways they have hurt you, begin to pray earnestly for the Lord to initiate the healing process. Approach them and tell them how hurt you are and why—this may scare you but it is worth the try. Whatever you decide to do, do not demand an apology, as this will only make matters worse!

If you are a parent and recognize that your relationship with your child or adult child is strained, I encourage you to approach them and invite them to express any pent up emotions they have regarding the way you hurt or wounded them.

Once you have invited your children to share their feelings, the process of reconciliation and restoration will be well under way. If you don't do this, they will continue to stuff their anger and bitterness towards you, resulting possibly with depression and in some cases thoughts of suicide. I have also noticed that adult children who don't tell their parents what they put them through end up frozen and unable to move forward into a career or field of interest.

Parents, if you have committed sins like adultery, were often drunk, or were harsh or abusive to your children, they will find it frightening to express how they truly feel about what you put them through. The best way to soften their fears is to let them know that you are genuinely sorry for hurting them and that you desire for your relationship to be reconciled and want them to be as honest as possible. Let them express their feelings; don't get defensive! After they share ask them if there is anything else they need to express. Once they say they have noth-

125

ing else to say, apologize. You will be amazed at how this simple act will improve your relationship with your child!

Another and perhaps safer option is for spiritual father and mother figures to stand in place of a wounded person's parents and apologize to them on their behalf. I have found that God breathes life into this option and have witnessed many receive healing.

A Mother Shares About Her Childhood

Earlier in chapter ten, "Different Ways Parents Unintentionally Wound Their Children," I shared how a woman in our church could not connect with her adult children because she had not been "mothered" by her mom because she was mentally ill.

This woman later received "mother heart" prayer from my wife for this issue and was powerfully healed by the Lord! She then sat down with her adult children and told them what her childhood was like. As she shared what she experienced as a child and how the Lord set her free, His presence flooded their living room and began to heal them! Tears flowed and strongholds lifted as they finally understood why their mother had not been able to emotionally connect with them the way they longed for her to do so!

In the days that followed, each of them sent e-mails to their mother apologizing to her for the ways they had judged her down through the years. Today this woman and her adult children are meeting twice a month to catch up on lost time. What the enemy had meant for evil, the Lord had worked out for their good (see Genesis 50:20)!

God is Turning the Hearts of the Parents

The Spirit of Elijah, one of thirty names of the Holy Spirit, is transforming families! Recently I watched three adult children fidget nervously as they waited for their father to show up at their children's home for a "family" meeting.

Their dad finally arrived and sat down with their mother to address them. What followed brought tears to my eyes as he expressed how sorry he was for having an extramarital affair with another woman when they were children. Incredibly he also shared that he could see how the affair had negatively affected each of their lives and gave each of them the opportunity to respond. One by one each of his adult children and wife shared how the affair had negatively impacted them and told him that they forgave him. They then each embraced one another in a tender moment that I will never forget!

Reconciliation Releases the Breakthrough!

When a parent humbles himself before his child and apologizes to him for any intentional or unintentional ways he hurt him, breakthrough is near! Parents, don't let fear or pride stop you from taking this important step. Reconciliation is high on God's agenda for your family so He will be there to help you!

Key Questions to Consider

If you are serious about being reconciled and restored to your family, I'd like you to take some time to consider the following questions:

1. What kind of person were you, in character, when your children were young (i.e., were you angry or impatient, stressed out or afraid, lonely or depressed, etc.)?

   Note: The reason why it is important for you to recall who you were, in character, when your children were younger is because they were impressionable at that time and didn't, because of their lack of experience, have the ability to understand what you were going through. This made them susceptible to the deceiver's lies; and as a result they came to false conclusions about themselves, you, and their relationship with you.

2. What was going on in your marriage when your children were younger (i.e., was your marriage falling apart or was it solid, were you quarreling a lot or were you at peace with your spouse, were you under financial stress, etc.)?

3. What conclusions did you draw about yourself and your parents when you were a child that carried over into the way you parented or related to your children?

4. Are you willing to endure emotional pain and relational discomfort to see your family healed and happy?

5. Are you willing to come clean about your past and admit how it impacted your children?

6. How have your past actions and attitudes impacted the way your adult children relate to each other today?

7. What relational patterns and emotional strongholds are your adult children dealing with today because of the decisions you made when they were younger?

If you answer these questions honestly, you will recognize how you failed your children. Although extremely difficult, this personal admission will prepare you for the next step, which is to take personal responsibility for how your actions and attitudes negatively affected your kids.

Remember, it is the truth that sets you free! (John 8:31–32). Don't hesitate! Don't put off your apology! If you wait until "the perfect time" to apologize, you may never do it!

In chapter twelve, "Ejection of Rejection," you will learn how the enemy launches the assignment of rejection upon your children and what you can do to help them overcome it.

Thoughts to Ponder

Chapter Eleven

1. The word translated *confess* literally means in the Greek language, "to agree with." When we confess our sins to one another and to God we are not taking God by surprise but are agreeing with Him that we have done wrong.

2. It takes humility to apologize to someone that we have injured. It takes courage to say, "I'm sorry, I was wrong, please forgive me."

3. Parents, don't let pride get in the way of apologizing to your children. Don't expect them to make the first move. You are the adults. Initiate the apology and watch God move!

4. In addition to pride, many parents do not apologize for the hurts they have inflicted upon their kids simply because they do not recognize the need to do so.

5. If you are a parent and you recognize that your relationship with your child or adult child is strained, I want to encourage you to go to them and invite them to express any pent up emotions, especially anger, regarding your relationship.

Small Group Discussion Questions

Chapter Eleven

1. Read James 5:16.

2. Describe any memory you have of your mom or dad apologizing to you for something they said or did to you that was wrong. What impact did their confession have upon you?

3. Read 1 John 1:9. What does the word *confession* mean? Have you ever had to "confess" something to someone else? If so, what was the experience like?

4. Read Proverbs 16:18 and 1 Peter 5:5. What are the consequences of being prideful?

5. Read Proverbs 28:13 and share about a time when you "covered" your sins instead of "confessing" them. What happened?

6. Pray for each other as God leads.

Ejection of Rejection

12

*For the Son of Man in his day will be like the lightning, which flashes and lights up the sky from one end to the other. But first He must suffer many things and be **rejected** by this generation.*
—LUKE 17:24–25

Rejected by My High School Sweetheart

Like all people my age, I used to be a lot younger. I won't tell you how old I am, but I will tell you that I was a senior in high school when John Travolta starred in the hit movie *Dance Fever*. That same year I met a woman (not my wife) who I thought I would marry. After a year and a half of going steady, she decided, to my great shock, to sever our relationship. Deeply wounded, I barely managed to finish my first semester in college as my soul ached from the sting of rejection.

It is easy to recognize rejection when someone we love severs ties with us. But most parents, I have observed, do not recognize how easily their children feel rejected when they yell at them, express disapproval about something they've done, or say something negative about their appearance or performance, etc.

Luke 17:24–25 tells us that Jesus was rejected by His people. He came to embrace the house of Israel but few embraced Him. Isaiah 53:3 predicted this:

He [Jesus] is despised and **rejected** of men; a man of sorrows, and acquainted with grief: and we hid as it were our faces from him; he was despised, and we esteemed him not.
—ISAIAH 53:3, KJV

There have been many books written about rejection and how it negatively impacts peoples' lives. A friend who specializes in deliverance ministry once said to me that it is his belief that the spirit of rejection is the primary weapon the devil uses to hinder God's people.

Years ago I was invited to minister prophetically at a prophetic conference in Honolulu. I was one of a dozen individuals who had been asked by the conference organizer to minister to church groups over a three day period.

Day one went well as the Lord released grace upon me to speak words of encouragement and edification over His people. As I walked toward my car after the first session, a pastor approached me with great urgency. After greeting me cordially, he expressed concern about an obscure issue that he felt would hinder my ability to prophesy over his people. I acknowledged his concern and encouraged him to speak to the conference organizer.

The next day I was shocked to learn that instead of going to the conference organizer as I had suggested, this pastor forbid his members from attending the session where I was scheduled to prophesy over forty members of his church! As I drove home that afternoon, the spirit of rejection began to creep into my soul. By late afternoon I was in tears and didn't want to return to the conference.

What is Rejection?

The Free Dictionary defines the word *reject* as: (1) To be unwilling to accept or recognize; (2) To refuse to grant or deny; (3) To throw out or discard.[1]

Rejection is a spiritual assignment from the pit of hell that negatively affects a person's mind, will, and emotions. The effect of this spiritual assignment affects not only the way a person relates to God but the way he relates to others and himself. The purpose of this chapter is to help parents understand how they unintentionally reject their children and what can happen as a result.

Rejection is a spiritual assignment from the pit of hell that negatively affects a person's mind, will, and emotions.

How Do Parents Reject Their Kids?

1. By making negative comments about their physical appearance and character

As I have already mentioned, my father was a Hungarian Jew and my mother a Japanese American. Being of mixed ethnicity, I felt that I was neither Jewish nor Japanese. This led to confusion about my identity, and I rejected the way God made me. My mother, who I am sure never intended to hurt me, would often comment how "fair" or "white" I was. Most of my friends at this time were darker in complexion. This led me to conclude that I didn't fit in because I had fair skin.

Parents, be careful not to give the devil the opportunity to launch the assignment of rejection against your children by making any negative comments about their appearance. The late Michael Jackson said in an interview in the year 2002 that his father, Joseph, repeatedly made derogatory comments about the shape of his nose and the condition of his skin (he had bad acne). These comments Jackson said, in the interview, wounded him so deeply that he dreaded performing on stage and wanted to die.

After watching this interview I finally understood why Michael Jackson had so many surgeries to alter the shape of his nose. He, like so many other children, had been rejecting himself because his father had made negative comments about his appearance.

2. By yelling or speaking harshly

Proverbs 12:18 says, "Reckless words **pierce** like a sword." In moments of tiredness and frustration many parents, myself included, have yelled at their children. Emotional outbursts such as these can potentially wound a child's self-esteem and over time cause them to close off their heart to their parents.

Parents, when you speak harshly to your kids they may conclude that you don't love them because they aren't experienced enough to know any different. And, of course, the devil will take advantage of every opportunity you give him to place the lens of rejection over the eyes of your child's heart.

3. By not recognizing the difference between immaturity and rebellion

Like many fathers, I have made my share of mistakes parenting my sons. Many of these mistakes have been because I wrongly perceived that my boys were rebelling against my authority when in actuality they were acting out of immaturity. If we parents would gently explain to our children why we want them to do certain things there would be far less drama in our homes. One of the worst things we can do is to tell our children, "It's my way or the highway!" Such outbursts accomplish nothing except to launch the assignment of rejection into our children's hearts!

Rebellion is defined as defiance against authority. *Immaturity*, on the other hand, is not being fully grown or developed. Don't assume when your child questions something you have asked him to do that he is rebelling against your authority. Instead, ask him questions to determine why he is questioning you. Talking to your children I assure you, will foster a healthy, ongoing relationship with them that will extend into their adult years. Of course, there will be times when discipline is absolutely appropriate (see Proverbs 23:13).

Remember, if you don't have a relationship with your kids, you cannot and will not be able to shape and influence them for the Lord. Parents, may you be like King David who said in Psalm 19:13, "Keep back your servant from **presumptuous** sins; Let them not rule over me; Then I will be blameless, And I shall be acquitted of great transgression" (NASB).

4. By favoring one child over another

Acts 10:34 tells us that God is not one to show partiality. Unfortunately, parents often favor one child over another, causing the child less favored to feel rejected. Like the Lord, we should not favor one child over another.

5. By being rigid and legalistic

In Jesus' day there was a group of religious leaders called the Pharisees. The Pharisees took it upon themselves to make sure everyone was following the laws of Judaism. This system of strict rules and regulations did not produce a society of people who loved God but a religious people who were critical and judgmental. Children who are raised in hyper spiritual homes that stress rules over loving one another and enforce the rules via "fear of punishment" are subject to the spirit of rejection because they repeatedly hear the message that keeping the rules is more important than accepting them, warts and all.

6. By constantly telling their children what they're doing wrong instead of what they're doing right

In Judges chapter 6 a young man named Gideon is threshing wheat at the bottom of a winepress to hide grain from the Midianites. Instead of berating Gideon for being timid and afraid, an angel of the Lord appeared to him and encouraged him:

> **Mighty hero**, the LORD is with you!
> —JUDGES 6:12, NLT

There's an old nursery rhyme that says, "Sticks and stones may break my bones but words can never hurt me!" This rhyme is simply not true because the words we say to our children have the potential to either tear them down or spur them on toward greatness! In Gideon's case, the angel of the Lord focused on who Gideon was in God not on his fears!

Parents, do you see your child's potential greatness or are you always harping on why they didn't do the dishes right, clean up their rooms better, get good enough grades, etc.? Here's a simple exercise to protect your children from rejection: Tell your kids ten things you have seen them do well this week. And, if they need correction about something they didn't do well, patiently explain to them how they can do that one thing better in the future. If you consistently practice this exercise, your children will not fall prey to the spirit of rejection.

135

7. By withholding love and affection

Children who do not experience their father and mother's love often deal with sexual identity issues. Confused, they long for their parents' approval, affirmation, and embrace.

If a boy does not receive his father's love in early childhood, he may seek intimacy with other men later in life. If a girl does not receive her mother's love in early childhood, she may do the same with other women. Moms and dads, if you shower your children with love and affection, they will not reject their sexual identity.

8. By passing on their own rejection issues

If a parent has experienced a lot of rejection, he may pass onto his child the lens of rejection. This lens is a way of relating to others based on the "fear" of being rejected by others. My mother for example, never received her father's blessing. He never told her that he was proud of her or affirmed her. Because of this, my mom grew up afraid to be honest with her feelings for fear that others would not accept her. Somehow I picked up my mom's fears and related the same way. Sadly, I grew up with few close friends because I was careful not to share my feelings with others. It was not until I matured in the Lord years later that I began to relate honestly.

What Are the Fruits of Rejecting Your Children?

1. Ungodly sources of love and acceptance

If a parent repeatedly rejects his child, his child will eventually seek out love and acceptance from a variety of ungodly sources in order to cope with his pain. These may include but are not limited to:

- Drugs and alcohol
- Gang involvement
- Relationships with the same sex
- Premarital heterosexual relationships

2. Low self-esteem

When a child does not feel loved or accepted by his parents, his potential is capped. Disappointed, lonely, and afraid, he will not venture out to "test the waters" but will stay where he perceives it is safe.

3. Unhealthy patterns of relating in the family line

A confident parent who has healthy self-esteem will reproduce confident children. But a parent who does not have healthy self-esteem will reproduce children who have low self-esteem.

Ejection of Rejection

If you want to eject rejection from your home, the first step is to "recognize" that you have been rejecting your child, even if unintentionally. This will be difficult, but once you do it your family will be on the pathway to healing.

Secondly, take personal "responsibility" for rejecting your child, even if it was unintentional. This step requires that you allow the Lord to soften and sensitize your heart to see things from your child's perspective not just your own.

Thirdly, go to your son or daughter and apologize for any ways you rejected them in the past. This step will pay massive dividends!

Fourthly, bless your kids! Affirm them for who they are not what they've done or not done. Tell them that they are special and that you are pleased with them.

Finally, tell the Lord that you are sorry for misrepresenting His heart to your children and thank Him for forgiving and cleansing you (see 1 John 1:9).

In chapter thirteen, "A Dad's Job Description" we will spell out the job description God has given to fathers.

Thoughts to Ponder

Chapter Twelve

1. Jesus came to embrace the house of Israel with love and compassion, but few embraced Him (see Luke 17:24–25; Isaiah 53:3).

2. *The Free Dictionary* defines the word *reject* as: (1) To be unwilling to accept or recognize; (2) To refuse to grant or deny; (3) To throw out or discard.[2]

3. Rejection is a spiritual assignment from the pit of hell that is sent to wound a person's soul (mind, will, and emotions).

4. Proverbs 12:18 says, "Reckless words pierce like a sword."

5. In Judges chapter 6 a young man named Gideon is threshing wheat at the bottom of a winepress to hide grain from the Midianites. Instead of berating Gideon for being timid and afraid, the angel of the Lord appeared to him and said, "Mighty hero, the LORD is with you!" (Judges 6:12).

Small Group Discussion Questions
Chapter Twelve

1. According to Merriam-Webster, what is rejection?

2. Describe an incident when you felt rejected? What happened? What did you conclude about yourself? Others? How did you overcome rejection?

3. In the section entitled "How Do Parents Reject Their Kids?" Pastor Rob lists eight ways parents unintentionally reject their children. Reread this list and share any insights about rejection that the Lord has revealed to you.

4. What are the fruits of rejection?

5. Do you need prayer for any rejection or self-rejection issues?

13

A Dad's Job Description

Then the LORD said to Moses, "Instruct Aaron and his sons to bless the people of Israel with this special blessing. 'May the LORD bless you and protect you. May the LORD smile on you and be gracious to you. May the LORD show you his favor and give you his peace.' This is how Aaron and his sons will designate the Israelites as my people, and I myself will bless them."
—NUMBERS 6:22–27, NLT

Unprepared to Be a Father

I spent:

- 7 years in grade school (K–6)
- 6 years in high school (7–12)
- 4 1/2 years in college earning a Bachelor of Arts degree
- 4 1/2 years earning a Masters of Divinity degree

With 21 years of education, one would think that I would have been at least somewhat prepared to be a father. The reality was, however, I had no clue how to be a father. When my wife gave birth to our first son, Jordan, I pitched in with changing his diapers, feeding him, and, of course, carrying him. Everything seemed awkward at first but I quickly got the hang of doing the "dad thing." My heart at the time was to help my wife, Barbara, by giving her occasional breaks. My vision for fatherhood at this time, however, was limited at best because no one had ever taught me how to be a father. Like every dad, I had to learn while on the job.

No Job Description

Prior to leaving for California to get my master's degree, I worked for a large medical insurer. Overall, I had a very good experience at this company except for the first two weeks. I say this because no one sat me down during this time to explain my job description to me. Finally, someone was assigned to help me learn what I needed to learn to do my job effectively and I was off and running. The purpose of this chapter is to define what the Bible says is a father's job description.

Obedience School

After leaving the medical insurance industry in 1987, my wife and I packed up our belongings and our twenty-month-old son, Jordan, and left for California to attend Golden Gate Seminary. Leaving Hawaii was difficult, as we had to say goodbye to our family and friends.

Among the other things that were difficult, was having to give away our one-year-old dog, Brandy. Brandy was a beautiful yellow Labrador Retriever. When we brought her home, we instantly fell in love with her. Quickly she grew to about sixty pounds of playful muscle. She would bounce around our yard and home like a rubber ball. It was challenging to control her, so we decided to take her to obedience school.

I showed up at obedience school at a local park in the community where we lived a week later, excited that our dog would soon be trained. I was in for a big shock as the obedience school trainer began to instruct each dog owner, not the dogs, how to handle their pets. This proved to be frustrating, as Brandy did not respond to any of my commands. Even more frustrating was that she instantly responded to the trainer's commands. It then dawned on me that Brandy wasn't the one getting trained, it was me; or should I say I was!

Parents who learn how to parent their children are far more effective at parenting than those who do not. (I strongly recommend the *Growing Kids God's Way* video series by Gary and Marie Ezzo.)

A Father's Job Description

There are six short verses in the Bible that outline a father's job description. They are:

> Then the LORD said to Moses, "Tell Aaron and his sons to bless the people of Israel with this special blessing: 'May the LORD bless you and protect you. May the LORD smile on you and be gracious to you. May the LORD show you his favor and give you his peace.' Whenever Aaron and his sons bless **the people of Israel** in my name, I myself will bless them."
>
> —NUMBERS 6:22–27

In this passage God instructs Moses to tell his brother Aaron, the high priest, how to bless the "children" of Israel. As a priest, Aaron was the spiritual father of God's family. This is why I believe that the Aaronic blessing is a type of job description for dads.

Father's are the conduits through whom God releases His blessing.

First: A Father's Most Important Job is to "Bless" His Children Regularly.

Father's are the conduits through whom God releases His blessing. In Genesis 31:13 God instructed Jacob to leave Paddam-aram and return to the land where he was born. In response to God's leading, Jacob gathered his family, livestock, and belongings and crossed the Euphrates River for Israel. His uncle Laban, whom Jacob had worked for over twenty years, was enraged that Jacob had left without saying goodbye and pursued him with vengeance in mind (see Genesis 31:22–23). Because Laban was a man with much authority, the Lord confronted him in a dream:

> Be careful that you **do not speak** to Jacob either good or bad.
> —Genesis 31:24, nasb

Eventually Laban caught up with Jacob in the hill country of Gilead and declared:

> **It is in my power to do you harm** [speak curses upon you], but the God of your father spoke to me last night, saying, "Be careful not to speak either good or bad to Jacob."
> —Genesis 31:29, nasb

Laban understood, as did every father in the Middle East, that his words carried the power to curse his children, grandchildren, and, in this scenario, his son-in-law. A father's blessing is of the utmost importance because it secures his children's future well-being—this is why Rebekah told Jacob to seek his father's blessing (see Genesis 27:18–29).

In Genesis 14:18–19 we read that Melchizedek, King of Salem, blessed Abram, saying, "**Blessed be Abram** by God Most High, Creator of heaven and earth" (v. 17). By blessing Abram, Melchizedek released not only prosperity upon him but upon his generational legacy. The following verses reveal how Melchizedek's blessing impacted Abram's generational legacy!

1. Abraham was **wealthy**!

> The Lord has blessed my master abundantly, and he has become **wealthy**.
> —Genesis 24:35

2. Isaac was **very wealthy**!

Isaac planted crops in that land and the same year reaped a hundred-fold, because the LORD had blessed him. The man became rich, and his wealth continued to grow until he became **very wealthy**!

—GENESIS 26:12–13

3. Jacob was exceedingly prosperous!

In this way the man [Jacob] grew **exceedingly prosperous** and came to own large flocks, and maidservants and menservants, and camels and donkeys.

—GENESIS 30:43

4. Joseph both fathered Pharaoh and ruled Egypt!

He [the Lord] made me [Joseph] father to Pharaoh, lord of his entire household and **ruler over all of Egypt**.

—GENESIS 45:8

Manasseh and Ephraim, the sons of Joseph, were **collectively the largest** of the twelve tribes of Israel totaling 85,200 men!

These were the clans of Manasseh; those numbered were **52,700**.

—NUMBERS 26:34

These were the clans of Ephraim; those numbered were **32,500**.

—NUMBERS 26:37

(Perry Stone speaks of this at some length in his book *Breaking the Jewish Code*, chapter 12, "Impart before You Depart.")[1]

The Second Aspect of a Father's Job Description is to Keep or "Protect" His Children.

This means that a father is to be aware of what is going on in his children's lives. Being aware means being involved. It means being in relationship with his children in order to know what they are facing (i.e., challenges, issues, pressures, etc.) Often this aspect of a father's job description is fulfilled by mothers because dads are "too busy" with work or their hobbies to be aware of their children's challenges.

Over the years I have had many discussions with my sons about what is suitable for them to watch on TV and at the movies, etc. My aim has never been to control them but to explain to them "why" certain things are not healthy for them to watch. My heart has been to train them how to think for themselves according to the Word of God, not to make decisions for them. More importantly, they have watched me "live" by example what I have encouraged them to do.

Over the years I have had discussions with my sons about topics ranging from what to watch on TV, how to treat the opposite sex, pornography, how to handle bullies, spiritual warfare, and more. The point here is that I have been "actively" involved. Dads, if you don't mentor your children, the world and all of its ungodly values will be their mentors. Such an approach spells "disaster." A son or daughter without a father to protect them will draw their own conclusions about life and themselves because no one is around to guide them.

Note: A special encouragement to single moms: You have the full backing of heaven as you raise your children! You are precious to the Lord! He knows the challenges you face having to be both father and mother. Do your best and His grace will cover the rest!

A Third Aspect of a Father's Job Description is to "Smile" Upon His Children.

Numbers 6:25 puts it this way:

The LORD make his face **shine** on you.

Dads, one of the best things you can do is tell your children how "pleased" you are with them! Be pleased with them not because of what they accomplish but because they are simply your children. In the movie *Iron Man 2*, starring Robert Downey Jr., Tony Stark, the lead character (aka Iron Man) watches an old film where his father, Howard Stark, shares about his vision for the future for his company. Up until this point in the movie, Stark believed that his father did not love him. Everything changed for Stark when his father broke down at the end of the film and said that his greatest achievement was not all his inventions but his son Tony! Stark is immediately inspired and invents a new power source that "saves the day!" Even a deceased father's words have the power to propel a son to achieve greatness!

Matthew the tax collector recorded in his Gospel a profound blessing spoken by God the Father over His Son:

This is My beloved Son, with whom **I am well-pleased**; listen to Him!
—MATTHEW 17:5, NASB

Fathers, do your children know that you are pleased with them? Have your kids felt the approval of your smile? Or have they experienced only the frown, what my oldest son calls "the look," of your disapproval? Dads, you have the power to empower your children to reach greater heights by simply expressing that you are pleased with them!

The Fourth Part of a Father's Job Description is to Be Gracious to His Children.

Our heavenly Father is a gracious God. Psalm 103:8–14 paints an amazing picture of the graciousness of our heavenly Father:

> The LORD is compassionate and **gracious**, Slow to anger and abounding in lovingkindness. He will not always strive with us, Nor will He keep His anger forever. He has not dealt with us according to our sins, Nor rewarded us according to our iniquities. For as high as the heavens are above the earth, So great is His lovingkindness toward those who fear Him. As far as the east is from the west, So far has He removed our transgressions from us. Just as a father has compassion on his children, so the LORD has compassion on those who fear Him. For He Himself knows our frame; He is mindful that we are but dust.
> —PSALM 103:8–14, NASB

Numbers 6:25b says, "...and be **gracious** to you." Dads, you have been called by God to be His ambassadors of grace. When you take this divine charge seriously, God will give you the grace to be gracious to your children. Like you, your kids will make many mistakes and need grace. You will impact them profoundly when you are slow to anger and abounding in lovingkindness!

In 2009 my youngest son, Jonathan, came home from school and reported, with great anxiety, that he had gotten into an accident and damaged his grandmother's car. Gently I told him that it was okay and that I was glad that he wasn't hurt. My mother's car could be replaced, but yelling at Jon would have only damaged his self-worth and our relationship.

The Fifth Aspect of a Father's Job Description is to Create an Environment of "Peace" or Security for His Children.

When a father is present, his children grow up secure and relatively unafraid. But when a dad is consistently or altogether absent from his children's lives, they are more likely to grow up fearful and insecure.

Fathers, your children need to know that you will never abandon them (see Hebrews 13:5). In an early chapter I shared that my youngest son, Jonathan, was hurt because I had stopped attending his soccer games to attend his older brother's baseball games. I am grateful to God that Jon, urged on by my wife, shared his feelings with me, because I had not taken into account his need for me to be standing on the sidelines at his games. I call this "father power!"

Father Power!

As I draw this chapter to a close, I would like to share two success stories of people whose lives have been changed as the result of "father power." By "father power" I am referring to the application of the job description presented in this chapter.

147

Success Story Number One

A man in his mid thirties shared how God led him to not take a lucrative job offer in California and remain in Hawaii to work with youth. Right after he declined the job offer, his dad called from New York and asked him if he could bless him. The man was surprised because his father had never blessed him before. This was a success story for two reasons: First, in response to the man's obedience not to take the job and work with youth, God gave him something far greater—his father's blessing. Secondly, the man's father had not practiced any of the seven aspects of a father's job description listed in Numbers 6:24–27. He had been selfish, harsh, and verbally abusive. But through divine intervention, this father was learning how to impact his son's life!

Success Story Number Two

During one of our Sunday worship services, a man in his forties approached me telling me that he urgently needed to speak with me. Not able to hear what he was saying because of the praise and worship going on, I motioned for him to follow me outside. Outside he lamented that he wanted to break free from drug addiction but just couldn't do it. After he finished sharing, I told him that God loved him and that I did too. I then asked him if I could hug him and speak a "father's blessing" over him. He agreed, and I wrapped my arms around him and blessed him with all of my heart knowing that his dad had abandoned him in childhood and that he had never been affirmed.

Tears ran down his cheeks as the Father tangibly poured His love into him. I would not see this man for another six months. "Great!" I thought. "That didn't work!" Then it was reported to me that this man had been put in jail and that while in prison his life had changed for the better!

Recently this man returned to church transformed in character, appearance, and spirit. Not only had God freed him from his addiction to drugs but God had impressed upon him the desire to serve. He shared with me that the turning point came when I had blessed him with a father's blessing! Praise God!

Dads, You Can Fulfill Your Job Description!

If you are a dad, I would like to encourage you to fulfill God's job description for you as a father! God has given you the authority to radically shape and impact your children today and their future tomorrow! If God is stirring you, drop to your knees and ask Him to grant you the grace you need to be the father He has called you to be!

In chapter fourteen, "Reaching Your God-Given Potential Is Possible," you will learn how to break free from the cultural constraints that hold you back from achieving God's plan for your life.

Thoughts to Ponder

Chapter Thirteen

1. Over the years it has been my observation that parents and particularly fathers who have learned how to parent their children are far more effective at parenting than those who have not.

2. The Aaronic blessing (see Numbers 6:24–27) is a type of job description for dads.

3. Single moms, you have the full backing of heaven as you raise your children! You are precious to the Lord! He knows the challenges you face having to be both father and mother. Do your best and His grace will cover the rest!

4. Dads, one of the best things you can do is tell your children how "pleased" you are with them!

5. Dads, you have been called by God to be His ambassador—to represent Him well to your children.

6. Dads, you have been given "father power" so use it for your children's good!

Small Group Discussion Questions
Chapter Thirteen

1. Read Numbers 6:22–27 from the perspective that it is a father's job description.

2. Review: Identify the five aspects of a father's job description.

3. Did your dad bless you? Protect you? Express his pleasure about you? Give you grace when you messed up? Create security? Lead you by personal example? Educate you about God's ways? Love on you? Be respectful as you share about your dad! Is there anything you need to forgive your dad for?

4. Dads, which of the five aspects of being a father do you feel like the Holy Spirit is nudging you to work on?

5. Pray for one another.

SECTION III
TRANSFORMING OUR LAND

14

Reaching Your God-Given Potential is Possible!

I can do everything through him who gives me strength.
—Philippians 4:13

Our Deepest Fear

Marianne Williamson, a Jewish spiritual teacher, author, lecturer, and philanthropist, wrote a paragraph in her book *A Return to Love*,[1] which describes the essence of the "Janteloven Stronghold" or "Small Man" syndrome that affects multiple cultures throughout Hawaii and the world:

> Our deepest fear is not that we are inadequate. Our deepest fear is that we are powerful beyond measure. It is our light, not our darkness that frightens us. We ask ourselves, who am I to be brilliant, gorgeous, talented and fabulous? Actually, who are you not to be? You are a child of God. Your playing small does not serve the world. There's nothing enlightened about shrinking so that other people won't feel insecure around you. We were born to make manifest the glory of God that is within us. It's not just in some of us; it's in everyone. And as we let our light shine, we unconsciously give other people permission to do the same. As we are liberated from our own fear, our presence automatically liberates others.[2]

Uncovering the Janteloven Stronghold

As mentioned in chapter two, "Understanding the Orphan Stronghold," a stronghold is a deeply ingrained attitude or mind-set that has a "strong hold" on a person influencing them to think, act, or relate in a way that is contrary to God's Word.

The Janteloven Stronghold is a cultural mind-set that affects how certain people groups perceive themselves and others. This stronghold expresses itself in many ways but is primarily identified when people believe that they are unable to

154

excel and reach their God-given potential.

The Janteloven or "Small Man" stronghold is not unique to Hawaiian Islands but is also found in other nations such as Australia, Canada, Chile, Japan, New Zealand, Norway, and Sweden.

The term *Janteloven* was first coined in 1933 by a Danish man named Aksel Sandemose. In that year Sandemose moved to Norway and discovered that many Norwegians were pessimistic and depressed. This led him to write a novel about a small Danish town, Jante, describing the thinking and unspoken rules he encountered while living in Nkyobing Mors.[3]

As Sandemose did research for his book he identified and recorded ten character traits that he observed not only in Nkyobing Mors but also throughout Norwegian culture. He then drew a parallel between the Ten Commandments and these ten character traits.[4] (The Norwegian name for the Ten Commandments is "Moseloven," literally "Law of Moses."[5])

The ten laws of Jante are:

1. Do not think you are anything special.
2. Do not think you are as good as we are.
3. Do not think you are wiser or smarter than we are.
4. Do not fool yourself into thinking you are better than we are.
5. Do not think you know more than we do.
6. Do not think you are more important than we are.
7. Do not think that you are good at anything.
8. Do not laugh at us.
9. Do not think that anyone cares about you.
10. Do not think you can teach us anything.[6]

The basic translation of these ten laws is clear: You aren't worth a thing! Who do you think you are? Nobody is interested in what you think! Mediocrity is your best bet! If you think and act in this way, others will not reject you! You are second-rate! Sure, God blesses people but you're not one of them! Of course God loves everyone, but you'll never get to be on His first team!

Origins

How did the Janteloven Stronghold make its way to the Hawaiian Islands? The Japanese have a proverb that says, "Deru kugi wa utareru," literally, "The stake that sticks out gets hammered down," or, "A tall tree catches much wind." The meaning of this is: if you stand out, you will be subject to criticism.[7] This means that a nonconformist will be pounded down and told "not to make waves" in order to maintain a posture of humility or more accurately "false humility." I believe that when Japanese immigrants landed on Hawaii's shores they brought with them this Janteloven thinking.

It is also possible that Hawaii may have been influenced by the Janteloven Stronghold via the United Kingdom, Ireland, Australia, and New Zealand. In these countries there is a "leveling" social attitude referred to as the "Tall Poppy Syndrome."[8] Someone is said to be affected by the Tall Poppy Syndrome as soon as he begins to succeed economically, socially, politically, etc., as others perceive him as presumptuous or attention seeking and "cut" him down.

In Hawaii you won't find many people talking about their accomplishment because this would be perceived as bragging or being "big headed!" To speak of your accomplishments in Hawaii or other cultures where the Janteloven Stronghold is present is to invite envy, rejection, and criticism from others.

Upon visiting a friend at the Hawaii State judiciary, I found him reading a magazine with his feet up on his desk. When I asked him if he was afraid of being reprimanded for "slacking" on the job, he replied that his "slacking" was expected by both his peers and supervisor. When I questioned him further about this, he explained that if he strived for excellence or did a better job than his peers he would be looked down on an even warned by his supervisor for making others look bad.

Playing Small

In her article "Hawaii's Oppression by Mediocrity," *Midweek* columnist Susan Page chronicled an experience she had in 1968 while teaching local teenage girls self-improvement:

> I was struck by how they [the girls] resisted shining, how they worked at "playing small." One girl always changed from grubby attire into her "class" clothes once she got there. Then after class she'd switch again, pulling her hair back in a tight ponytail and taking off any remnants of makeup before joining her friends. "Shame," she said, when I asked her why she didn't want to show-off her new improved look to her friends and family. This was my first experience with her being "fabulous" or even merely above average, was considered a bad thing.[9]

My Own Experience

When looking back to my high school years, I experienced first hand the Janteloven Stronghold on my first day of school. Having been raised by parents from the East Coast, I was not shy about sharing what I thought. So when my teacher asked if anyone would like to share, I quickly volunteered an answer. After being affirmed by my teacher for a good answer, I was met by the cold and angry "stink eye" by my new classmates. From that day forward I no longer raised my hand in class for fear of not being accepted by my peers. My desire for acceptance was so strong that I suppressed my God-given ability to speak out.

It is unfortunate that many of our children feel a sense of "shame" for getting good grades, raising their hands to volunteer an answer, or wearing nice clothes. From the day God created us, He intended us to succeed! Instead, many of our youth are capped and are not reaching their potential as adults. Sadly, the decision not to rise up and reach their potential is not influenced by the Prince of Peace but by the prince of darkness.

From the day He created us, God intended us to succeed!

Breaking Free from the Janteloven Stronghold

Although there is no formula for breaking free from the Janteloven Stronghold, there are steps you can take to unlock yourself from its grip:

1. Revelation

In order to overcome the Janteloven Stronghold you must recognize that you have been thinking and relating according to its laws. Once you come to this realization, you have taken the first step towards being set free.

2. Confession

To confess something to God is to "agree" with Him that you have been living and relating in a manner that does not line up with His will for your life.

3. Renunciation

To renounce something is to "break legal ties" with the very thing that has had a grip upon your life. This literally means taking a "strong hold" over the stronghold that has been negatively influencing you. This is accomplished by "renouncing" the laws of the Janteloven Stronghold that have kept you and your generational line in chains!

4. Forgiveness

To forgive others is to no longer hold against them the harm they have caused you. To forgive someone is to let go of the hurt, anger, and disappoint you have towards them. Forgiveness also means asking God to forgive you for hurting

157

Him, others, and yourself.

5. Truth

To break free completely from a stronghold requires more than confession, renunciation, and forgiveness. It requires incorporating a "new normal" into your thoughts and actions. This means making the choice to live by truths that acknowledge that you are special and have the potential to accomplish God's plan and purpose for your life.

6. Pray

Second Corinthians 10:4 states, "The weapons we fight with are not the weapons of the world. On the contrary, they have **divine power** [prayer] to demolish strongholds." Prayer moves the heart of God to "break through" on our behalf! The following prayer will help you to break free from the Janteloven Stronghold.

Thank You, Lord, that You have revealed to me that I have lived much of my life under the influence of the Janteloven Stronghold. Because of this revelation, I come into agreement with You that I need to be freed from its negative influences. I now renounce the Janteloven Stronghold and its many forms, including the spirits of false humility, passivity, lethargy, religiosity, conformity, mediocrity, rebellion, apathy, legalism, judgmentalism, envy, jealousy, and the anti-prophetic spirit. Today I declare that these ungodly influences will no longer hinder me from obeying Your call for me to break free, rise up, and become the son (or daughter) you have called me to become!

Lord, I now renounce each of the ten laws of the Janteloven Stronghold:

1. I renounce, break, shatter, and destroy the mind-set that I am not special! The truth is I am a person of great worth because I am created in the image of God and because Jesus chose to go to the cross on my behalf!

2. I renounce, break, shatter, and destroy the mind-set that I do not have the same standing as others. The truth is I have been created equal by God with all men and because Jesus destroyed the dividing wall between all ethnic groups, Jew and Gentile, when He died on the cross!

3. I renounce, break, shatter, and destroy the mind-set that others are smarter or wiser than I am. The truth is I have the wis-

dom of the Holy Spirit living within me and am able to access it by simply asking for it.

4. I renounce, break, shatter, and destroy the mind-set that I am not better than others. The truth is God has a plan and purpose for my life and has set me up to be a winner!

5. I renounce, break, shatter, and destroy the mind-set that others know more than I do. The truth is, because of the Spirit's transforming presence in my soul, I am full of knowledge!

6. I renounce, break, shatter, and destroy the mind-set that others are more important than I am. The truth is I am equally as important with all men or Jesus would not have laid down His life for me. God therefore honors me as much as anyone!

7. I renounce, break, shatter, and destroy the mind-set that I am not good at anything. I break the belief that I am a "jack of all trades but a master of none" and reject the lie that "noble deeds are done in silence." The truth is the Spirit of God has distributed to me unique gifts and talents for the blessing and benefit of others!

8. I renounce, break, shatter, and destroy the mind-set that no one can laugh at me. The truth is that God the Father loves me and fully embraces me as His son or daughter. Because I am accepted as I am by God what others think or say about me need not control me (this includes people laughing at me)!

9. I renounce, break, shatter, and destroy the mind-set that no one cares about me. The truth is that God the Father crowns me with lovingkindness, tenderness and mercy!

10. I renounce, break, shatter, and destroy the mind-set that no one can teach me anything. The truth is that I have a teachable spirit and am open to learn from whomever God places in my life!

How Does the Jante Law Match Up with God's Word?

Jante Law

1. Do not think you are anything special.
2. Do not think you are as the same standing as us.
3. Do not think you are wiser (or smarter) than we are.
4. Do not fool yourself into thinking you are better than we are.
5. Do not think you know more than we do.
6. Do not think you are more important that we are.
7. Do not think you are good at anything.

8. Do not laugh at us.

9. Do not think anyone cares about you.

10. Do not think you can teach us anything.

God's Word

1. You are a chosen people, a royal priesthood, His own special people (see 1 Peter 2:9).
2. Before God you are the same standing as all people (see Ephesians 2:14–18).
3. God's wisdom is available to every believer (see James 1:5).
4. If you obey God's commands you will be the head and not the tail (see Deuteronomy 28:13).
5. Through His word God wants to give you knowledge and purpose (see Proverbs 1:4).
6. You are so important to God that He sacrificed His Son on your behalf (see Romans 8:32).
7. God has given you specific gifts and talents to bless others (see 1 Corinthians 12:7–11; 1 Peter 4:10).
8. If someone laughs at you forgive them and move on (see Ephesians 4:32).
9. Not only does God care about you but He has placed you in a spiritual family that will love and care for you no matter what (see 1 Peter 5:7; Romans 12:10).
10. God has called you to be discipled and then to do the same for the nations of the earth (see Matthew 28:19–20).

Rise Up

The Janteloven Stronghold is a group-centered cultural stronghold that subtly influences God's people, via the fear of rejection, not to take hold of their God-given purpose and destiny. This stronghold creates a legalistic spirit that makes people uncomfortable with celebratory worship. It transforms delight into religious duty and grateful service into work and obligation! People under the influence of the Janteloven Stronghold are capped. Because their emotions are capped their worship is capped.

The Janteloven Stronghold is a group-centered cultural stronghold that subtly influences God's people, via the fear of rejection, not to take hold of their God-given purpose and destiny.

This stronghold pressures others to conform or face rejection. It neutralizes what the Spirit of God declares about an individual's destiny. It levels everyone off so that no one shines above others. It causes people to believe they are not special, important, or good at anything. It causes them to resist the spirit of prophecy and to question their value to God and others. May the Lord pull this stronghold down in your life! May He uncap you so you can soar into your God-ordained destiny! May you rise up and take your place in God's house, the world, and the marketplace!

In chapter fifteen, "Transforming Our Land One Family at a Time," we will visualize and examine God's dream for our land.

Thoughts to Ponder

Chapter Fourteen

1. The spirit of false humility downplays the compliments and encouragement of others, minimizing your accomplishments in God.

2. A passive spirit influences an individual to "hold back" instead of "step out."

3. A lethargic spirit leads one to take the "path of least resistance" instead of "persevere."

4. A religious spirit tries to conform others to unspoken rules with the threat of rejection and nonacceptance.

5. A spirit of conformity discourages creativity, diversity, and achievement perpetuating "mediocrity."

6. The spirit of rebellion leads believers to rebel against spiritual authority. Spiritual authority is given to leaders to build up the Body of Christ. Rebellion is launched against God's people to get them to mistrust authority.

7. The spirit of apathy influences you not to care about the needs of others.

8. The spirit of legalism monitors others' actions, breeding "the fear of man."

9. The anti-prophetic spirit is a spirit that resists those who speak destiny and purpose over peoples' lives.

10. The spirit of envy leads believers to become insecure and angry because they perceive that others are "getting ahead" of them.

Small Group Discussion Questions

Chapter Fourteen

1. Take turns reflecting on Marianne Williamson's statement in the introduction of this chapter.

2. In your own words define the Janteloven Stronghold.

3. Review the ten laws of the Janteloven Stronghold and then share which one has personally affected you and why.

4. What spoke to you most after reading this chapter?

5. What do you really think when someone shares with you a recent success?

6. Is it easy or difficult for you to tell others that you are doing well?

7. Do any of you believe you need to pray the prayer to break free from the Janteloven Stronghold? If so, pray the prayer provided in this chapter.

15

Transforming Our Land One Family at a Time

*Tell the whole community of Israel that on the tenth day of this month each man is to take a lamb **for his family, one for each household**. If any household is too small for a whole lamb, they must share one with their nearest neighbor, having taken into account the number of people there are.*
—Exodus 12:3–4

Set Free

After hearing His people cry out in desperation for help, God set in motion His plan to set them free from Egyptian captivity. He implemented this plan by telling Moses and Aaron to instruct every father in the community of Israel to slaughter a one-year-old lamb without defect. Each father was also told to take some of the lamb's blood and brush it on the sides and tops of the door frames of their homes (vv. 5–6).

At midnight the Angel of the Lord descended upon Egypt bringing God's judgment on their gods including the firstborn of their households (v. 29). But when God saw the lamb's blood sprinkled on the doorposts of each of the Israelite's homes He passed over them (v. 23).

One Family at a Time

The Passover story is widely recognized in the Judeo-Christian community as a story of great deliverance, as 1.5 million Israelites were set free from the most powerful nation in the ancient world by the blood of the Lamb!

Just as the Israelites were set free from their chains, people who have applied the blood of the Lamb, Jesus Christ, to the door posts of their hearts have been set free from Satan's chains. Just as the Lord transformed the lives and circumstances of 1.5 million people, He wants to do the same in our generation! How will this happen? One family at a time!

166

God not only set 1.5 million slaves free, He loosed individual families! He set the families free by providing a lamb for each household. And for those families that were unable to afford a lamb, He urged larger families within the Israelite community to invite them over to their homes to celebrate the Passover.

The Lord is a "big" God with a big agenda, but He is not too big not to notice and care for one family at a time! The blood of Jesus, the Passover Lamb, was shed for your family in order to redeem or deliver you from what has kept you in bondage.

> Now to him who **is able to do immeasurably more** than all we ask or imagine, according to his power that is at work within us.
> —EPHESIANS 3:20

Adopt One Family at a Time

Can you imagine what God could do in the region of the world where you live if every believing family adopted another family and introduced them to Jesus via simple acts of kindness and prayer? Can you imagine how your life would change if you stepped out of your comfort zone and shared the Lamb of God with another family? Can you imagine the impact you would have if you did the same at your office or workplace?

The Blind Side

Sandra Bullock received an academy award for best actress for her starring role in the movie *The Blind Side*. In this movie based on a true story, Bullock befriends Michael Oher, a teenager who has already been in foster care with several families. Every time Michael is sent to a new home he runs away.

One afternoon as Leigh Anne Tuohy (played by Sandra Bullock) is driving home, she notices Michael walking along a road shivering in the cold. Filled with compassion, she offers him a ride and a place to spend the night. The next morning Leigh Anne invites Michael to spend Thanksgiving Day with her family. He accepts and from that day forward he and the Tuohy family develop a lasting bond.

The Blind Side opened in 3,110 theaters on the weekend of November 20, 2009. It grossed $34,510,000! The movie enjoyed a very rare greater success for the second weekend than it did in its opening weekend, taking in an estimated $40 million.[1]

Psalm 68:5–6 says, "Father to the fatherless, defender of widows—this is God, whose dwelling is holy. God places the lonely in families; he sets the prisoners free and gives them joy" (NLT). I believe *The Blind Side* is a modern day snapshot of how the family of God, if activated, can impact the Michael Ohers of this world. This movie was a box office smash because everyone, like Leigh Ann Tuohy, wants to make a difference in this world!

Individuals throughout the Body of Christ are positioned today, like Leigh Ann Tuohy and her family, to help transform other people's lives!

Individuals throughout the Body of Christ are positioned today, like Leigh Ann Tuohy and her family, to help transform other people's lives! The question is not, "Can this happen?" but, "Are we willing to cooperate with the Spirit of God?"

Supernatural Help is Yours!

Throughout this book I have referred to the ministry of the Holy Spirit as He manifests Himself as the spirit of Elijah. Let's revisit Luke 1:13–17 one last time:

> But the angel said to him: "Do not be afraid, Zechariah; your prayer has been heard. Your wife Elizabeth will bear you a son, and you are to give him the name John. He will be a joy and delight to you, and many will rejoice because of his birth, for he will be great in the sight of the Lord. He is never to take wine or other fermented drink, and he will be filled with the Holy Spirit even from birth. Many of the people of Israel will he bring back to the Lord their God. And he will go on before the Lord, in the spirit and power of Elijah, to turn the hearts of the fathers to their children and the disobedient to the wisdom of the righteous— **to make ready a people for the Lord."**

The spirit of Elijah rested on John the Baptist as he called the nation of Israel, parents, and children to turn their hearts back to one another. This amazing forerunner ministry "prepared" Israel for the first coming of Jesus. Many know that Jesus is coming a second time, but few realize that the spirit of Elijah has been released in every part of society to prepare us for that glorious day:

> Jesus replied, "To be sure, **Elijah comes** and **will restore** all things. But I tell you, Elijah has already come, and they did not recognize him, but have done to him everything they wished."
> —MATTHEW 17:11–12

Jesus states here that Elijah, or His cousin John the Baptist, had preceded him but that Elijah would come again. Before Jesus returns a second time a great awakening will occur in our land as the spirit of Elijah sweeps through God's house worldwide and in the marketplace restoring fathers and mothers to their children and vice versa. Those who do not yet know the Lord will be swept into the Kingdom of God as individuals seek answers and help for the challenges they face in their families. I want to be a part of this, don't you?

In chapter sixteen, "God Wants to Change Your Name," you will discover that God wants to first heal your dysfunction and then catapult you into your destiny!

Thoughts to Ponder

Chapter Fifteen

1. Can you imagine what God would do in the region of the world where you live if every believing family adopted another family and introduced them to Jesus via simple acts of kindness and prayer?

2. Can you imagine how your life would change if you stepped out of your comfort zone and shared Jesus with another family? With a co-worker or fellow businessman?

Small Group Discussion Questions

Chapter Fifteen

1. How many of you have seen the movie *The Blind Side*? What did you like about the movie? Did God challenge you at all when you watched it? If so, how?

2. Who do you know that isn't a believer yet that you could invite over to your home for dinner? Pray for? Bless?

3. Write down the names of three people (or families) you have a heart for. Spend your remaining group time asking the Father to reveal Himself to them.

4. Commit yourselves to pray for three people for thirty days. After thirty days of prayer, invite them out for lunch or coffee to hang out. When the Lord opens the door, offer them prayer for any "felt" needs they have. When God provides for their "felt needs" explain why God has done this for them.

5. Have one or two people practice sharing their personal testimony.

16

God Wants to Change Your Name

*You are the LORD God, who chose **Abram** and brought him from Ur of the Chaldeans and **renamed him Abraham**.*
—NEHEMIAH 9:7, NLT

From Dysfunction to Destiny

In chapter one of this book I shared with you the story of how God began to reveal Himself to me as loving Father when an Argentine woman declared, "You're God's bambino!" In the years that followed that divine encounter, the Lord began the process of removing from my heart the stones and rocks of dysfunction (see Isaiah 57:14; 62:10) that blocked me from knowing Him as Daddy.

God is first and foremost a loving Father. Knowing God cannot be intellectual alone but must also be experiential. This is why the apostle Paul wrote:

And may you have the power to understand, as all God's people should, how **wide**, how **long**, how **high**, and how **deep** his love really is.
—EPHESIANS 3:18, NLT

As I began to see and experience God as my Father, everything began to change. I was no longer an insecure, driven man bent on achieving things for God but a son resting in His Father's love and strength. As I began to see and relate to my Father with new eyes, He began to release more of His favor upon my life, moving me toward my destiny in Him.

God not only wants to reveal Himself to you as Father but He also wants to move you toward your preordained purpose and destiny!

God not only wants to reveal Himself to you as Father but He wants to

174

move you toward your preordained purpose and destiny! Now some of you may be thinking, "Why would God pick me? For one thing I am unqualified, and for another, I am too messed up!" My friend, the words of the apostle Paul should excite you because you are exactly the kind of person that the Lord chooses. Check it out in 1 Corinthians 1:28–29:

> God chose **things despised** by the world, **things counted as nothing at all**, and used them to bring to nothing what the world considers important, so that no one can ever boast in the presence of God.
> —1 Corinthians 1:28–29, nlt

What's in a Name?

You are God's workmanship (Ephesians 2:10)! He chose you! This is why the Father works overtime to heal you so He can reveal Himself to others through you! This transformational process includes changing your destiny. Throughout the Bible God changed people's destiny by changing their names. A person's destiny was linked to the name that God gave them. A person's purpose was "in" their name.

A person's purpose was "in" their name.

I Will Change Your Name

In the late 1980s my wife, Barbara, and I were a part of a church called Mount Tam Community Church in Marin County, California. One of the praise choruses that Mount Tam loved to sing was "I Will Change Your Name," written by D.J. Butler and published by the Anaheim Vineyard in 1987. I love this song because it captures God's heart to pull people out of their dysfunction and thrust them into their God-ordained purpose. The lyrics are:

> I will change your name
> You shall no longer be called
> Wounded, outcast, lonely or afraid
>
> I will change your name
> Your new name shall be
> Confidence, joyfulness, overcoming one
> Faithfulness, friend of God
> One who seeks My face.

When God changes your name, He changes your identity. When you know your identity as a son or daughter, you will walk in your authority.

When God changes your name, He transforms you from a wounded, outcast, lonely, and fearful person into an individual who is confident, full of joy, able to overcome adversity, faithful, and who walks in His divine purpose.

Abram to Abraham

The Bible records the names of several individuals that God renamed in order to alter their purpose and destiny. These individuals were people through whom the Lord chose to accomplish His eternal purposes.

In Genesis 12:1–3 we read of how God first appeared to a seventy-five-year-old man named Abram. Abram means "exalted father" which was ironic at the time because Abram and his wife Sarai were childless.

Twenty-four years later the Lord appeared again to Abram and told him that He was changing his name to Abraham which means "father of many nations" (Genesis 17:3–5). By changing his name God altered Abram's destiny, setting in motion a generational legacy that is still being perpetuated today!

God grabbed a seventy-five-year-old man with no heir and promised him that all the peoples of the earth would be blessed through him! Abraham pursued his God-given dream for his life with great faith until it came to pass as recorded in Genesis 21:2! Today millions of believers have a relationship with God the Father because the "father of many nations" believed God when He said, "I am changing your name. It will no longer be Abram; now you will be known as Abraham, for you will be the father of many nations" (Genesis 17:5)!

Sarai to Sarah

Sarai, the wife of Abram, accompanied her husband as he left the comfort of his father's household in Haran for the land of Canaan (see Genesis 12:1, 4–5). According to Genesis 12:2 Abram and Sarai left the known for the unknown because Abram believed that the Lord would make him into a great nation.

In the natural, Abram's decision to leave his father's tent made no logical sense because Sarai was unable to have children (see Genesis 16:1). Like Rachel, Hannah, and Elizabeth (see Genesis 30:1; 1 Samuel 1:4–8; Luke 1:5–7), Sarai faced the sociocultural stigma of her day because she was barren. Interestingly, Sarai means "mockery."

Later Sarai convinced Abram to sleep with her maidservant Hagar in order to jumpstart their family (Genesis 16:1–4). Once Hagar became pregnant Sarai began to despise her: "When she [Hagar] knew she was pregnant, she began to despise her mistress. Then Sarai said to Abram, 'You are responsible for the

176

wrong I am suffering. I put my servant in your arms, and now that she knows she is pregnant, **she despises me**'" (vv. 4–5).

I cannot imagine the emotional torment Sarai endured. In spite of this, God fulfilled His promise to Abraham and appeared to him unexpectedly when he was ninety-nine years old and declared:

> As for Sarai your wife, **you are no longer to call her Sarai; her name will be Sarah.** I will bless her and will surely give you a son by her. I will bless her so that she will be the mother of nations; kings of peoples will come from her.
>
> —GENESIS 17:15–16

The Lord changed Sarai's name to Sarah—Sarah means "princess." In a moment the Lord changed the course and destiny of Sarah's life. She would no longer be mocked for her inability to conceive but would be recognized as the mother of nations!

Jacob to Israel

The name Jacob literally means "supplanter," "he grasps at the heel," or "he deceives." In Genesis 27:36 we read that Jacob lived up to his name by stealing both his brother's birthright and blessing. In spite of his shortcomings and failures God still pursued Jacob because He had a greater plan for his life.

I have come to conclude that once you begin to understand that God loves you and that you are His favored child, everything will to shift for you! In order for you to grasp this revelation, God will reveal Himself to you in a new way. He often does this through the language of dreams. This was how He revealed Himself to Jacob:

> Jacob left Beersheba and set out for Haran. When he reached a certain place, he stopped for the night because the sun had set. Taking one of the stones there, he put it under his head and lay down to sleep. **He had a dream** in which he saw a stairway resting on the earth, with its top reaching to heaven, and the angels of God were ascending and descending on it. There above it stood the LORD, and he said: "I am the LORD, the God of your father Abraham and the God of Isaac. I will give you and your descendants the land on which you are lying. Your descendants will be like the dust of the earth, and you will spread out to the west and to the east, to the north and to the south. All peoples on earth will be blessed through you and your offspring. I am with you and will watch over you wherever you go, and I will bring you back to this land. I will not leave you until I have done what I have promised you." When Jacob awoke from his sleep, he thought, "Surely the LORD

is in this place, and I was not aware of it." He was afraid and said, "How awesome is this place! This is none other than the house of God; this is the gate of heaven." Early the next morning Jacob took the stone he had placed under his head and set it up on a pillar and poured oil on top of it. He called that place Bethel, though the city used to be called Luz. Then Jacob made a vow saying, "If God will be with me and will watch over me on this journey I am taking and will give me food to eat and clothes to wear so that I return safely to my father's house, then the LORD will be my God and this stone that I set up as a pillar will be God's house, and of all that you give me I will give you a tenth."

—GENESIS 28:10–22

Jacob's encounter with God was so powerful that he worshipped the Lord and promised to give Him a tenth of all his future earnings! Jacob, remember, means "He deceives." God looked beyond Jacob's many shortcomings and renamed him "Israel," meaning "He shall be prince of God" or "He struggles with God and prevails." Jacob "the deceiver" became Jacob "the ruler":

After Jacob returned from Paddan Aram, God appeared to him again and blessed him. God said to him, "Your name is Jacob, but you will no longer be called Jacob; **your name will be Israel**." So he named him Israel.

—GENESIS 35:9–10

Jacob, the grandson of the Patriarch Abraham, became the father of a nation because God changed his name!

Ben Oni to Benjamin

Rachel was the love of Jacob's life. She bore him his eleventh son, Joseph. Jacob was elated when Rachel became pregnant again with their second child. But Jacob's world shattered when Rachel pushed her son into the world and died. In a moment of sadness before she died, Rachel named her son Ben-Oni or "son of my sorrows," but Jacob renamed him Benjamin or "Son of my right hand" (see Genesis 35:16-18).

God did not personally change Ben-Oni's name but I believe He led Jacob to change it. I believe God led him to change his name because the name Rachel had selected for her son was not in sync with God's plan for Benjamin's life. If Benjamin had been named Ben-Oni, his life surely would have been filled with sorrow. But because his father renamed him "Benjamin" the direction and course of his life was altered. Such is the power of a father's words!

Benjamin's descendants became fierce warriors (see Genesis 49:27) and generations later produced the apostle Paul (Romans 11:1)! This all occurred because of a simple yet profound name change!

Joseph to Zaphenath-paneah

Rachel named her firstborn son Joseph, meaning "May the Lord give me yet another son" (Genesis 30:24). Rachel knew nothing of the plans God had for her baby boy—that one day he would save not only the twelve Patriarchs of Israel but also the nation of Egypt and other nations as well.

At the appointed time (see Psalm 105:19–22), Joseph was made ruler over Egypt by Pharaoh who renamed him Zaphenath-paneah or "savior." Zaphenath-paneah (savior) was strategically positioned to save many from a terrible famine:

> The seven years of abundance in Egypt came to an end, and the seven years of famine began, just as Joseph had said. There was famine in all the other lands, but in the whole land of Egypt there was food. When all Egypt began to feel the famine, the people cried to Pharaoh for food. Then Pharaoh told all the Egyptians, "Go to Joseph and do what he tells you." When the famine had spread over the whole country, Joseph opened the storehouses and sold grain to the Egyptians, for the famine was severe throughout Egypt. **And all the countries came to Egypt to buy grain from Joseph, because the famine was severe in all the world.**
>
> —Genesis 41:53–57

Joseph was able to save his father's entire household, the future nation of Israel, and the nations that surrounded Egypt because God had changed his name!

Saul to Paul

The apostle Paul is perhaps the greatest if not the best known believer in the New Testament. Before he became known as Paul, however, he was known as Saul of Tarsus (see Acts 13:9). The name Saul means "asked for" or "requested by the people," referring to that time in Jewish history when the Israelites asked God for a king (see 1 Samuel 8:6).

When writing to the Philippians, Paul shared what used to be a source of tremendous pride—his past success when he was known as Saul:

> I could have confidence in my own effort if anyone could. **Indeed, if others have reason for confidence in their own efforts, I have even more!** I was circumcised when I was eight days old. I am a pure-blooded citizen of Israel and a member of the tribe of Benjamin—a real

Hebrew if there ever was one! I was a member of the Pharisees, who demanded the strictest obedience to the Jewish law. I was so zealous that I harshly persecuted the church. And as for righteousness, I obeyed the law without fault.

—Philippians 3:4–6, nlt

Acts 9:3–4 tells us how the Lord changed Saul's destiny:

As he [Saul] was nearing Damascus on this mission, a brilliant light from heaven suddenly beamed down upon him! He fell to the ground and heard a voice saying to him, "**Saul, Saul!** Why are you persecuting me?"

—Acts 9:3–4, nlt

Saul of Tarsus was transformed during this supernatural encounter with the Lord! Sometime between Acts 9:3–4 and Acts 13:9, Saul became known as Paul. The name Paul means "little," "small," or "humble."

It is not known exactly when God changed Saul's name to Paul, but it doesn't matter; because when Saul became Paul, God began to move through him in a mighty way. Paul's might, however, was not rooted in his own strength but in God's, as the Lord transformed him from a man who prided himself in his many accomplishments into a "humble" or "small" servant.

Saul viciously persecuted God's people (see Acts 8:1; 1 Timothy 1:12–13). God changed his name to "little" and redirected the course of his entire life. Paul himself tells us in 1 Corinthians 2:1–5:

When I first came to you, dear brothers and sisters, I didn't use lofty words and impressive wisdom to tell you God's secret plan. For I decided that while I was with you I would forget everything except Jesus Christ, the one who was crucified. I came to you in **weakness—timid and trembling**. And my message and my preaching were very plain. Rather than using clever and persuasive speeches, I relied only on the power of the Holy Spirit. I did this so you would trust not in human wisdom but in the power of God.

—1 Corinthians 2:1–5, nlt

Paul's life, destiny, and direction were altered because God changed his name!

From Orphan to Son

As I sat in a counseling room at Elijah House in Post Falls, Idaho, I shared with my counselor a dream I had had hours before. In this dream I explained that I was on a skateboard powering myself up a hill. In the next scene, I told her that I was going into a gondola (cable car) and then in a moment the gondola surged with power and was lifted, with me in it, up a steep mountain.

After sharing this dream with my counselor, I stopped and asked her, "What does it mean?" She looked at me and said, "God has brought you to Elijah House to take you off the mountain of performance and to transfer you into the gondola of His grace! From this day forward God will take you up the mountain of the Lord!"

For the next four days I wept over and over as my counselor ministered to the multiple orphan structures that lay underneath the depression that had gripped my life. I left Elijah House that week with new hope in my heart! I left Post Falls no longer an orphan but a son! As my wife and I returned home to Hawaii from Idaho, we knew that God had shifted our lives and ministry to a new place and a new direction! We were now in the gondola of our heavenly Father's grace and we were going up!

Since our return from Elijah House, we have seen God move miraculously in our marriage, our family, our finances, and our ministry! The point here is not to draw attention to ourselves but to encourage you that God can heal you of your dysfunction and move you into your purpose and destiny! God can change not only your name but the course and direction of your life!

9/11 Wake-up Call

Who can forget that awful day on September 11, 2001, when terrorists attacked the Pentagon in Washington DC and the World Trade Center in New York City, killing over 3,000 people! I was jolted out of my bed at 3:45 a.m. on that day by the sound of my phone ringing. Half asleep I staggered out to my living room and picked up the phone. When I held the phone to my ear, there was no voice on the other end. "A prank call," I thought to myself and stumbled back to bed.

As I was about to go back to sleep, I realized that I had just had a vivid dream. In this dream I saw a tunnel of chaos filled with smoke and debris with people screaming and running frantically in every direction. As I sat on my bed pondering the dream, I had no idea that terrorists had just crashed airplanes into the World Trade Center and the Pentagon. Tired, I went back to bed.

Three hours later I got up and turned on the TV. Like those across our nation, I was shocked to see the World Trade Center engulfed in flames. The dream now made perfect sense. I realized, later, that my phone had rung at the exact time that the Pentagon had been attacked.

The tragedy of 9/11 was more than an attack on our nation! It was a wake-up call for God's people! We are a sleeping giant that needs to be awakened! Romans 8:19 says:

> For all creation is **waiting eagerly** for that future day when God will reveal who his children really are.
>
> —Romans 8:19, nlt

The church, as you know, is not the building we go to but the family of God. All of creation is waiting for us to arise! This awakening will occur as the Father continues to unveil Himself to the present and next generation. This will occur as God raises up spiritual fathers and mothers who will release their spiritual children into their purpose and destiny and earthly fathers and mothers who will represent the Father to their children in the way He has always wanted them to. This will occur as God removes our dysfunction and we become sons and daughters instead of orphans. And this will occur as we do our part to showcase Jesus in the marketplace and the world!

Are you ready for God to change your name? If you are, bow your head right now and give your heavenly Father permission to change your name, your identity, and your destiny! It won't be easy but it will be the best decision you ever make!

In the seventeenth and final chapter, "Restoring Our Hearts to Our Jewish Fathers," we will address how God is restoring the church to its Jewish foundations and how this will release worldwide harvest!

Thoughts to Ponder

Chapter Sixteen

1. God is first and foremost a loving Father. Knowing God cannot be intellectual alone but must also be experiential (see Ephesians 3:18).

2. God not only wants to reveal Himself to you as Father but He also wants to move you into your preordained purpose and destiny (see 1 Corinthians 1:28–29).

3. You are God's workmanship (Ephesians 2:10)! You are His choice! He works overtime to heal you so He can reveal Himself to others through you!

4. The tragedy of 9/11 was more than an attack on our nation! It was a wake-up call for God's people (see Romans 8:19).

5. As God removes our dysfunction we will become sons and daughters instead of orphans.

Small Group Discussion Questions
Chapter Sixteen

1. Where were you on September 11, 2001?

2. What do you think your heavenly Father thinks about you? If God the Father was talking to one of His angels about you right now, what would He be saying? Why?

3. Respond honestly to the following statement: God the Father loves you the same way He loves His Son the Lord Jesus! Do you believe this? Why or why not?

4. This chapter discusses how God changed several Bible figures' names and therefore their destinies. Which story (i.e., Abram to Abraham, Sarai to Sarah, Ben Oni to Benjamin, Jacob to Israel, Joseph to Zaphenath-paneah, Saul to Paul) spoke to you the most? Why?

5. Share briefly how God has changed your name (identity) and therefore your purpose (destiny). If you haven't experienced this yet, ask those present to pray for God to anchor you in the reality that you are His precious son or daughter.

Restoring Our Hearts to Our Jewish Fathers

17

Listen to me, all who hope for deliverance—all who seek the LORD! Consider the quarry from which you were mined, the rock from which you were cut! **Yes, think about your ancestors Abraham and Sarah, from whom you came.** *Abraham was alone when I called him. But when I blessed him, he became a great nation.*
—ISAIAH 51:1–2, NLT

My Dad

My dad, the late Bertram Gross, was a Hungarian American Jew who grew up in Yonkers, New York at the turn of the twentieth century. Although a Jew, my father did not pass on to me anything about his religious beliefs or practices. Because of this, I grew up in Hawaii totally unaware of my Jewish heritage. Little did I know that twenty-seven years after my father's death God would turn my heart to both my Jewish roots and the Jewish people!

City Reaching Conference

In the fall of 2001 my wife, Barbara, and I attended Harvest Evangelism's annual city reaching conference in Buenos Aires, Argentina. This week-long conference was full of new revelation about God's desire to disciple not only individuals but entire cities. Toward the end of the conference, my wife and I attended a Harvest Evangelism luncheon hosted by a Messianic Rabbi from Kazakhstan. The luncheon, we were told, was about reaching Jerusalem.

Certain that the Lord wanted us to attend the luncheon, my wife and I walked into the room where it was held with a sense of anticipation and excitement. As soon as we sat down next to the Rabbi, we could hardly contain ourselves from bursting into tears. What, we asked ourselves, was God up to?

As we ate our lunch with other conference attendees, the Rabbi shared from the Scriptures that Jerusalem was chief among the cities that the Lord intended to reach. He finished his presentation and then a Harvest team representative named Miguel Sanchez stood up and asked if any of us were Jewish. A few

186

of us, including myself, raised our hands. Miguel then asked if we would walk to one side of the room. My wife and I walked to the other side of the room.

What followed changed our lives. As those of us of Jewish ancestry stood facing the other luncheon attendees, Miguel said that He felt led by the Lord to ask us for forgiveness. I can't recall specifically what Miguel and the others repented for, but I do remember weeping as God's presence tangibly touched us.

As I was weeping, the Rabbi came by and laid his hands on me, saying, "Lord, release the well of Jewishness in this man all the way back to Abraham, Isaac, and Jacob! Instantly, I burst into tears and could not stop crying for the next thirty minutes. It was one of the most powerful "God encounters" I have ever had!

After being showered with God's blessing in Argentina, my wife and I returned to Hawaii. Not realizing the deep implications of what God had released upon us through the Rabbi we focused on pastoring our church.

In the weeks and months that followed, the Lord spoke to me through several dreams. In one dream I stood at my father's grave holding a Torah scroll with a prayer shawl wrapped around my shoulders and yarmulke on my head. In a second dream the Lord beckoned me to step into a pool of Jewishness, while in a third dream I was reaching out to Jewish people in my community.

The obvious finally made sense to me—God was connecting me to my Jewish roots. In the years that followed God gave me insight about Shabbat (the Sabbath), the power of blessing our children, the feasts of Israel, and much more.

The Church is Awakening to its Foundations!

In the past decade there has been an awakening, of sorts, in the church. This awakening has been focused on Israel, Jews, and Judaica (Jewish literature, religious icons, and other items related to Judaism). Today it is not uncommon to see believers wearing Jewish prayer shawls (*talit*), blowing Jewish ram horns (*shorfarim*) and applying anointing oils from Israel when praying for the sick.

In addition to the growing interest in Jewish things, Don Finto's book *My People Shall Be Your People*, and Robert Heidler's book, *The Messianic Church Arising*, have provided a biblical framework for understanding God's heart and end-time purposes for the Jewish people.

So why is God generating all of this interest about Israel and the Jewish people? God is releasing revelation to the church about Israel and the Jewish people because He intends to restore the church to its Jewish foundations! In Ephesians 2:11–22 Paul tells us that when Jews in Messiah and Gentiles in Christ become the "one new man" (v. 15, NKJV), God will dwell with the church:

> Consequently, you [Gentiles] are no longer foreigners and aliens, but fellow citizens with God's people and members of God's household, built on the foundation of the apostles and prophets, with Christ Jesus himself as the chief cornerstone. In him the whole building is joined together and rises to become a holy temple in the Lord. And in him **you too are being built together to become a dwelling** in which God lives by his Spirit.
>
> —EPHESIANS 2:19–22

In order to understand the "One New Man," Gentiles (non-Jews) need to see from God's vantage point that the Jews are a part of His family. In Acts 7:38 God refers to the Israelites as "the church" in the desert (wilderness):

> This is that Moses who told the Israelites, "God will send you a prophet like me from your own people." He was in the **assembly** in the desert, with the angel who spoke to him on Mount Sinai, and with our fathers; and he received living words to pass on to us.
>
> —ACTS 7:37–38

The Hebrew word for assembly is **kahal**, which is translated "**ecklessia**" in the Greek version of the Old Testament. The word assembly is also translated in different Bible versions as "**congregation**" or "**church.**"

Most of us know that the church was birthed on the Day of Pentecost (see Acts 2:1) when tongues of fire rested on 120 believers in an upper room on Mount Zion. But most believers do not realize that the "Old Testament" church was also birthed on the Day of Pentecost, but on Mount Sinai as the Lord's presence also descended as fire (see Exodus 19:18).

On Mount Sinai the Lord gave 1.5 million Jews, who had just been freed from 430 years of Egyptian slavery, "living words" to follow (see Acts 7:38). On Mount Zion the Lord infused 120 Jewish believers with His Spirit. In effect, two families were birthed on the Day of Pentecost but on different mountains in different centuries. One family received His Word while the other received His Spirit.

Roots

As a young boy, Alex Haley first learned of his African ancestor Kunta Kinte by listening to the family stories of his maternal grandparents while spending his summers in Henning, Tennessee. According to family history, Kunta Kinte landed with other Gambian Africans in "Naplis" (Annapolis, Maryland), where he was sold into slavery.

Alex Haley's quest to learn more about his family history resulted in his writing the Pulitzer Prize winning book *Roots: The Saga of an American Family*. The book has been published in thirty-seven languages, and was made into the first week-long television miniseries, viewed by an estimated 130 million people.[1]

We Are Rooted in Abraham and Sarah

Every believer, whether Jewish or non-Jewish, can trace his spiritual roots all the way back to Abraham and Sarah. They are, according to Isaiah 51:1–2, the quarry from which each of us were mined and the rock from which each of us were cut. Although it is nice to know that our origins are traceable to Abraham and Sarah, we must still ask the question: Why does this matter? Because I am Jewish I would like to answer this question by asking another question: How can a tree (the Gentile church) bear the fruit God wants it to bear without its Jewish root system?

We Have Drifted from Our Roots

Several years ago I was invited by a friend to go snorkeling off the shores of Diamond Head beach on Oahu. Although I had snorkeled a lot in my youth, I hadn't gone snorkeling in over thirty years. Because of this I decided to shadow my friend closely as we entered the water.

As we waded out into the ocean, we began to look for fish to spear. Wanting to stick close to my friend, I repeatedly raised my head out of the water to make sure he was nearby. I was able to stay behind him for awhile until I got sidetracked by the beauty of the reef below.

Half an hour later I realized that I hadn't checked on my friend's whereabouts. When I lifted my head out of the water, he was nowhere to be found. My anxiety increased when I realized that I had drifted far from the shore into deep waters. At this point I began to hear the soundtrack of the movie *Jaws* in my head and quickly swam back toward the shoreline to safety.

Just as I drifted away from my friend, the church has drifted, for centuries away from its Jewish foundation (roots). When I say Jewish foundations or roots I am referring to our spiritual forefathers: Abraham, Isaac, and Jacob.

Divine Nourishment Comes from Our Forefathers

It is common knowledge that, except for a small number of Jewish converts in the first century, the majority of Jews rejected Yeshua (Jesus) and the Good News. When the Jews rejected the Gospel, Jesus did not panic but instead exercised plan B (see John 10:16), directing His followers to proclaim the Kingdom of God to

189

the Gentile world.

The worldwide Gentile family of God numbers in the hundreds of millions today because the Jews rejected the message of Messiah (Christ) crucified. According to Paul, however, non-Jewish believers must be careful not to overlook the spiritual reality that if it were not for the Jews and their forefathers the Patriarchs (Abraham, Isaac, and Jacob) they would not have received the blessings of the Gospel. Let's examine Paul's thoughts on this matter in Romans 11:17–18:

> If some of the branches [first century Jews who rejected the Gospel] have been broken off and you [Gentiles], though a wild olive shoot, have been grafted in among the others [the entire family of God down through the centuries] and now share in the nourishing sap [the life-giving blessings from the patriarchs or Jewish forefathers] from the olive root, do not boast [be arrogant towards] over those branches [the Jews who rejected the Gospel]. If you do, consider this: You do not support the root [the patriarchs], **but the root [the patriarchs] supports you.**

Flowing up to every Gentile from the root system of the Patriarchs is a "life-giving sap" that contains the covenant promises of Abraham.

Membership Has its Privileges!

In my teens I had a close friend whose father was a member of a country club. Being members of this club meant that my friend's family had certain privileges, such as being able to play golf whenever they wanted to, dining at the country club restaurant, swimming in the club pool, and much more.

Because Gentiles (non-Jewish believers) have been grafted into the olive tree of Israel, they are able to access the benefits of being a member or citizen of Israel. In Romans 9:4–5 Paul tells us how God blessed the Jewish people:

> Theirs [the people of Israel] is the adoption as sons; theirs the divine glory, the covenants, the receiving of the law, the temple worship and **the promises.** Theirs are the patriarchs, and from them is traced the human ancestry of Christ, who is God overall, forever praised! Amen.

In Ephesians 2:11–13 Paul explains that because of Christ's finished work on the cross, non-Jewish believers are family members or citizens of the commonwealth of Israel having become beneficiaries of the covenant promises of God.

A Promise is a Promise

Soon after my wife and I planted Mountain View Community Church in 1992, a woman with bipolar disorder (manic depression) became a member of our

190

church. Two years later this woman informed me that she was going to commit suicide. I pleaded with her not to do this but she would not be swayed.

Before saying goodbye she asked me to promise her that I would look after one of her three adopted adult daughters who was also a part of our church family. I told her that I would and she hung up.

Several days later I received a phone call from the woman's husband informing me that his wife had overdosed on pain medications and died. Over the past decade I have been true to my promise and have looked after her daughter.

You Have Access to the Covenants of Promise

When God makes a promise, it is called a covenant. A covenant is a divine agreement, oath, treaty, or guarantee sealed in blood. In Ephesians 2:13 Paul stated "But now in Christ Jesus you [Gentiles] who once were far away **have been brought near** [into the commonwealth of Israel] by the **blood of Christ**."

Prior to His death on the cross Jesus, along with His twelve disciples, celebrated the Passover as they reclined at a table and ate together. It was during this intimate gathering that Jesus "**sealed the deal with a meal**" (see Luke 22:7–20).

The next day Jesus was crucified and a new covenant was permanently established in His blood. By sealing this covenant, Jesus not only made it possible for all people to become children of God (see John 1:12–13) but for all non-Jews to become the recipients of every covenant promise God made to Abraham (see Galatians 3:29). What are these covenant promises?

1. The promise to make Abraham the father of a great nation (see Genesis 12:2a).

   This promise was fulfilled in 1948 when the United Nations voted to officially make Israel a member of the international community.

2. The promise to bless or prosper Abraham (see Genesis 12:2b).

   This promise was fulfilled many times during Abraham's life as he owned livestock, silver and gold, camels, and had many servants (see Genesis 12:16; 13:2; 20:14–16; 24:34–35).

3. The promise to bless those who blessed Abraham and curse those who cursed him (see Genesis 12:3c).

4. The promise to make Abraham a blessing by blessing all the families (and nations) of the earth through him (see Genesis

12:3b; 18:18; 22:18).

5. The promise to give the land of Canaan to Abraham's offspring (see Genesis 12:7; Psalm 105:8–11).

This promise was also fulfilled in 1948, when the land
became a Jewish nation again after nearly 2,000 years of
being ruled by others.[2] By giving Abraham's offspring
land, the Lord made it possible for them to raise livestock, grow crops, discover water, mine precious metals
and minerals, build cities, and much more!

6. The promise to greatly multiply Abraham's descendants as
the dust on the earth, the stars in the sky and the sand on the
seashore (see Genesis 13:14–16; 15:5; 22:17).

This promise has been fulfilled and continues to be
fulfilled today as millions of people have received Jesus
Christ as their personal Lord and Savior (see Galatians
3:7–9, 14, 29).

7. The promise to make Abraham the father of not just one nation but a multitude of nations (see Genesis 17:4–5).

The Secrets of His Covenant

One of the major reasons I believe the Lord is releasing revelation and understanding to the church about its Jewish foundations is so it can learn to access the
covenant promises He made to Abraham, Isaac, and Jacob.

Psalm 25:14 says:

Friendship with the LORD is reserved for those who fear him. With
them he shares **the secrets of his covenant**.

—PSALM 25:14, NLT

Those who have great respect for the Lord are His friends and are permitted to come into His presence and glean from His counsel. The word translated
secret in the verse above means couch or cushion and paints the picture of a circle
of friends sitting together having an intimate conversation. God desires to help
His friends understand the gracious provisions contained in His covenant. God
allows those who love Him to see and understand that they can access the covenant blessings He released upon Abraham, Isaac, Jacob, and their descendants.
Contained within each of the promises God made to the Patriarchs is not only
financial success but relational, physical, emotional, and spiritual success as well.
Collectively, these promises define what biblical "prosperity" is all about.

How Do We Tap into the Covenant Blessings of the Patriarchs?

The "nourishing sap" that flows from the patriarchal roots of Israel to us today is activated when fathers pray blessing over their children. In Genesis 48 we read where Joseph, the great-grandson of Abraham, heard that his father's (Jacob's) health was declining and he visited him with his two sons Manasseh and Ephraim. Joseph not only wanted to say goodbye to his father before he died but also wanted his father to "bless" his sons, as he clearly understood the impact his father's blessing would have on them. As Jacob's favorite son (see Genesis 37:3–4), Joseph had spent hours with his father in his tent hearing how his grandfather Isaac's blessing had significantly impacted the entire course of his father's life. Knowing this, he sought his father's blessing for his sons. Let's pick up the story in Genesis 48:2–20:

> When Jacob was told, "Your son Joseph has come to you," Israel rallied his strength and sat up on the bed. Jacob said to Joseph, "God Almighty appeared to me at Luz in the land of Canaan, and there he blessed me and said to me, 'I am going to make you fruitful and increase your numbers. I will make you a community of peoples, and I will give this land as an everlasting possession to your descendants after you.' Now then, your two sons born to you in Egypt before I came to you here will be reckoned as mine; Ephraim and Manasseh will be mine, just as Reuben and Simeon are mine. Any children born to you after them will be yours; in the territory they inherit they will be reckoned under the names of their brothers. As I was returning from Paddan, to my sorrow Rachel died in the land of Canaan while we were still on the way, a little distance from Ephrath. So I buried her there beside the road to Ephrath" (that is, Bethlehem). When Israel saw the sons of Joseph, he asked, "Who are these?" "They are the sons God has given me here," Joseph said to his father. Then Israel said, "**Bring them to me so I may bless them.**" Now Israel's eyes were failing because of old age, and he could hardly see. So Joseph brought his sons close to him, and his father kissed them and embraced them. Israel said to Joseph, "I never expected to see your face again, and now God has allowed me to see your children too." Then Joseph removed them from Israel's knees and bowed down with his face to the ground. And Joseph took both of them, Ephraim on his right toward Israel's left hand and Manasseh on his left toward Israel's right hand, and brought them close to him. But Israel reached out his right hand and put it on Ephraim's head, though he was the younger, and crossing his arms, he put his left hand on Manasseh's head, even though Manasseh was the firstborn. Then he blessed Joseph and said, "May the God before whom my fathers Abraham and Isaac walked faithfully, the God who has been my

shepherd all my life to this day, the Angel who has delivered me from all harm—may he bless these boys. **May they be called by my name and the names of my fathers Abraham and Isaac, and may they increase greatly on the earth**." When Joseph saw his father placing his right hand on Ephraim's head he was displeased; so he took hold of his father's hand to move it from Ephraim's head to Manasseh's head. Joseph said to him, "No, my father, this one is the firstborn; put your right hand on his head." But his father refused and said, "I know, my son, I know. He too will become a people, and he too will become great. Nevertheless, his younger brother will be greater than he, and his descendants will become a group of nations." He blessed them that day and said, "**In your name will Israel pronounce this blessing: 'May God make you like Ephraim and Manasseh.'**" So he put Ephraim ahead of Manasseh.

A Blessing for the People of Israel

According to the account above, Jacob gathered his strength and blessed his newly adopted sons, Ephraim and Manasseh. This short, obscure prayer has been spoken by Jewish fathers over their sons for centuries around the dinner table during the weekly Sabbath celebration while Genesis 24:60 and Ruth 4:11 have been spoken by fathers over their daughters.

Don't miss this: Jacob declared that the people of Israel would use the names of his adopted sons Ephraim and Manasseh to bless each other:

So Jacob blessed the boys that day with this blessing: "**The people of Israel will use your names to bless each other**. They will say, 'May God make you as prosperous as Ephraim and Manasseh.'"
—GENESIS 48:20, NLT

Note: Remember that Romans 11:17 and Ephesians 2:11–13 say that because you (Gentiles or non-Jews) have been grafted into the olive tree (Israel) you are now a citizen of the commonwealth of Israel. This means that you can enjoy the same blessings that God promised to the holy root of Israel (the Patriarchs). It means that if you are a father (or single mom) you can bless your children on a weekly basis with the same blessing contained in Genesis 48:20 and 24:60. If you do this your children "will" prosper!

In Isaiah 58:13–14 we read:

Keep the Sabbath day holy. Don't pursue your own interests on that day, **but enjoy the Sabbath** and speak of it with delight as the LORD's holy [special] day. Honor the LORD in everything you do, and don't follow your own desires or talk idly. If you do this, the LORD will be

your delight. I will give you great honor and give you **your full share of the inheritance** I promised to Jacob [see Genesis 27:28–29; 28:3–4; 29:13–15], your ancestor. I, the LORD, have spoken!
—ISAIAH 58:13–14, NLT

Jacob knew the "**secrets of God's covenant**" (see Psalm 25:14) because his father Isaac had blessed him multiple times! Because of this he had become exceedingly prosperous (see Genesis 30:43)! Like their forefathers Isaac and Jacob, Jewish fathers have tapped into the secrets contained in God's covenant and pronounced the blessings contained in Genesis 48:20 and 24:60 (and Ruth 4:11) over their children for thousands of years. As a result, the Jewish people, who constitute only one percent of the human race, have prospered unbelievably.[3]

Note: Read *Legacy of Blessing* to learn how to celebrate the weekly Sabbath and pray blessing over your children (copies can be purchased on Amazon. com). If you are concerned about becoming legalistic about the Sabbath, don't. Remember: You don't have to celebrate the Sabbath, you get to!

Why Ephraim and Manasseh?

Ephraim, which means "God has made me **fruitful** in the land of my suffering," was Joseph's second son while Manasseh, which means "God has made me **forget** all my troubles and the family of my father," was Joseph's first son (see Genesis 41:50–51). For thousands of years Jewish fathers have used these names to pronounce Jacob's blessing over their sons. This raises the question: Why Ephraim and Manasseh?

The answer can be summed by one word: *unity*. Ephraim and Manasseh are the only two brothers in the Book of Genesis who did not quarrel or fight. By contrast Abram and Lot fought (see Genesis 13:5–8); Ishmael mocked Isaac (see Genesis 21:8–10); Esau hated Jacob (see Genesis 27:41–45), and the sons of Jacob hated Joseph (see Genesis 37:3–4, 18–28).

Again, there is no biblical record of Ephraim and Manasseh ever being at odds with one other in any way. They were the epitome of brothers who dwelled together in perfect unity. We know from Psalm 133:1–3 that the Lord commands His blessing on brothers who dwell in perfect harmony. This is the reason why I believe Jacob chose Ephraim and Manasseh as the names by which the people of Israel would pronounce blessings on each other.

As a brief side note, Ephraim and Manasseh symbolize the "one new man" described in Ephesians 2:11–22 because Ephraim and Manasseh's parents were both a Jew and a Gentile. Joseph was a Jewish groom and Asenath, Joseph's wife, was a Gentile bride. God says in Ephesians 2:11–22 that His presence will dwell with the "one new man"—that He will command the blessing of His presence upon brothers who live together in perfect unity (see Psalm 133:1–3)!

Exercising the Secrets of God's Covenant Works!

Since writing *Legacy of Blessing*, a book about how to bless your family around the dinner table, many people have told me that they have seen God bless their children in amazing ways! Recently I received an e-mail from a woman who shared:

> My husband and I have been using the premise of your book and have been praying a parent's blessing over our son regularly over the last year. The results have been tremendous! His faith in coming back to life and recently he was one of three students accepted to a PhD program at Princeton fellowship that covers tuition, living expenses, and research—a blessing that came his way unexpectedly from the Lord.

This woman's e-mail is but one of many examples of how God's people can be blessed by simply tapping into the covenantal promises that flow from the root of Israel (the Patriarchs) to Gentile families. It is my prayer that all Gentiles will discover their Jewish roots and experience the blessings of Abraham, Isaac and Jacob!

Final Thoughts

Throughout this book I have alluded to Malachi 4:5–6 which states:

> Look, I [God] am sending you the prophet Elijah before that great and dreadful day of the LORD arrives. His preaching will turn the **hearts of the fathers to their children, and the hearts of the children to their fathers**. Otherwise I will come and strike the land with a curse.
> —MALACHI 4:5–6, NLT

These two power-packed verses about fathers and their children closed the Old Testament. They were the last written words God spoke for over 400 years. These verses, we have learned throughout this book, contain keys that will set families free from the negative influences of fatherlessness.

Malachi 4:5–6 contains revelation that goes beyond healing fathers and their children. I submit to you that this short passage contains another key that will heal nations! In order to identify this key, let's reread Malachi 4:5–6 with new lenses:

> See, I [God] am sending you the prophet Elijah before that great and dreadful day of the LORD arrives. His preaching will turn the hearts of the [**Jewish**] fathers to their [**Catholic, Greek Orthodox, and Protestant**] children, and the hearts of the [**Catholic, Greek Orthodox,**

196

and Protestant] children to their [**Jewish**] fathers. Otherwise I will come and strike the land with a curse.

God will turn the hearts of the Jewish people back to the hearts of their spiritual children—the Gentiles—and vice versa. I don't know how or when this will occur, but I know it will. I say this with confidence because:

1. Romans 11:23 tells us that God is able to graft the Jews back into their own olive tree!

2. Romans 11:25–26 states that once the full number of Gentiles (non-Jews) receive Jesus as their Lord and Savior all Israel will be saved!

3. Romans 11:28–29 says that God will save Israel because He loved their forefathers the Patriarchs (Abraham, Isaac, and Jacob) and because His gifts and call (of the Jewish people) are irrevocable!

Just as God desires to reconcile orphans into sons and daughters, He also desires to reconcile the Gentile church to its spiritual forefathers, the Jews. Let the celebration begin!

Thoughts to Ponder

Chapter Seventeen

1. In the past decade there has been an awakening, of sorts, in the church. This awakening has been focused on Israel, Jesus, and Judaica (Jewish literature, religious icons, and other items related to Judaism).

2. So why is God generating all of this interest about Israel and the Jewish people? God is releasing revelation to the church about Israel and the Jewish people because He intends to restore the church to its Jewish foundations.

3. Every believer can trace his or her spiritual roots all the way back to Abraham and Sarah. They are, according to Isaiah 51:1–2, the quarry from which each of us were mined and the rock from which each of us were cut.

4. How can a tree (the Gentile church) bear the fruit God wants it to bear without its root system?

5. Flowing up to every Gentile from the root system of the Patriarchs is a life-giving sap that contains the covenant promises of Abraham.

6. The "nourishing sap" that flows from the patriarchal roots of Israel to believers today can be activated when fathers pray blessing over their children.

7. Don't miss this: Jacob declared that the people of Israel would use the names of his adopted sons, Ephraim and Manasseh, to bless each other (see Genesis 48:20).

8. Ephraim and Manasseh are the only two brothers in the Book of Genesis who did not quarrel or fight.

Small Group Discussion Questions

Chapter Seventeen

1. Read Isaiah 51:1–2.

2. What do you know about your family line beyond your grandparents? If you know anything, please share what you know about your family heritage.

3. Abraham and Sarah are every believer's spiritual great-great-great-etc.-grandparents. They're the rock from which every believer is cut. Read Romans 11:17. Based on this verse, why is it important for every believer to know about his spiritual heritage?

4. Read Genesis 12:1–3; 13:14–16; 15:5; 17:4–5; 18:18, and 22:17–18. What did God promise to give Abraham?

5. Read Ephesians 2:11–13. According to these verses every believer is a citizen of Israel and has access to the covenant blessings promised by God to Abraham—reflect on this for a minute and respond.

6. Read Romans 11:17 and Ephesians 2:11–13 one more time. Then read Genesis 48:20. How can a Gentile (a non-Jewish believer) tap into the blessings promised to Abraham and the nation of Israel?

7. Recommendation: Read Legacy of Blessing.

8. Pray for one another as the Spirit leads.

Closing Thoughts

Thousands of years ago the Lord led Moses and the children of Israel out of Egyptian bondage to the front of Mount Sinai (see Exodus 19:1–2). Scholars have estimated that somewhere around 1.5 to 2 million Israelites camped at the foot of this mountain. The question is, why did the Lord lead this massive group of newly freed slaves into the Sinai?

Just as we are set free from the captivity of our sin so we can enjoy being God's sons and daughters, God set the Israelites free from 430 years of Egyptian captivity so they could enjoy being His children too! Not surprisingly, however, the children of Israel turned down God's invitation to "come up higher" and meet with Him (see Exodus 20:18–19). I say, "Not surprisingly," because the Israelites had been slaves for over four centuries.

Slaves or orphans, as we have learned in this book, lack basic trust and fear intimacy with father figures because they were abused, mistreated, or not "fathered" at all. Because the Israelites needed to be "fathered," God drew them to Mount Sinai to introduce Himself only to see them reject His invitation to "know" Him. They turned God down because they feared intimacy with Him and the unknown—this is why the Israelites repeatedly wanted to go back to Egypt where they wouldn't have to trust anyone.

Throughout this book I have emphasized that is God's heart to heal our land by releasing the spirit of Elijah upon each generation (see Malachi 4:5–6). As I draw this book to a close, it is my heart to call and challenge you to be a part of the "Elijah Task"! If our communities, towns, and cities are to be transformed, our families must first be transformed! If we fail to recognize this, our children (our legacy) will perish!

In Isaiah 39:5–7 Isaiah the prophet prophesied to King Hezekiah saying:

Hear the word of the LORD Almighty: The time will surely come when everything in your palace, and all that your fathers have stored up [Hezekiah's generational blessings] until this day, will be carried off to Babylon [exile]. Nothing will be left, says the LORD. And some of your descendants [Hezekiah's legacy], your own flesh and blood who will be born to you, will be taken away, and they will become eunuchs [Hezekiah's generational line will come to an end] in the palace of the King of Babylon.

Then Hezekiah replied in verse 8,

"The word of the LORD you have spoken is good." Hezekiah replied. For he thought, "There will be peace and security in my lifetime."

If we do not respond to the spirit of Elijah in this hour, our legacy (our children) will be carried off to Babylon and, worse yet, be completely cut off! Dads, may we not be like King Hezekiah who failed to heed the word of the Lord by concluding, "There will be peace and security in my lifetime." Instead, may we be like our spiritual forefathers—Abraham, Isaac, and Jacob, who recognized their responsibility to "father" the present generation well so that future generations could walk not only in greater blessing but their God-given destiny!

Appendix

Mother-Father Questionnaire

NAME_____

BIRTH ORDER_____

Questions:

1. Have you had a recurring or recent dream lately?

_____
_____
_____
_____
_____
_____

2. How can I help you?

_____
_____
_____
_____

3. What was or is your mom like? Was or is she loving, nurturing, kind, etc.? Withdrawn, harsh, fearful? On autopilot, controlling? Why?

_____
_____
_____
_____
_____
_____
_____

4. What was or is your relationship with her like?

_____
_____
_____
_____
_____
_____
_____

5. What was or is your dad like? Abusive, absent, authoritarian, passive, performance-oriented, good? Why?

_____
_____
_____
_____
_____
_____
_____
_____

6. What was or is your relationship with your dad like?

_____
_____
_____
_____
_____
_____
_____
_____

7. Did your parents pour into you (instruct, teach, counsel, coach, help, etc.)? In other words, who raised you?

_____
_____
_____
_____
_____
_____
_____
_____

8. Did anything traumatic happen in your family like the death of a child? Divorce? Loss of a job? Abandonment? Arguing? Rejection? Etc.? How did this affect your parents? You?

_____
_____
_____
_____
_____
_____
_____
_____

9. Can you recall anything that either your mom and/or dad did

or said that really hurt you? Why did it hurt you? Can you recall anything you wanted your parents to do for you but they didn't do it? How did this affect you?

_____
_____
_____
_____
_____
_____
_____

10. Did you conclude anything about yourself as the result of the hurtful event or things said? Did you conclude anything about your parents?

_____
_____
_____
_____
_____
_____

11. Judgments: Can you remember judging your parents for anything they said? Did or didn't do?

_____
_____
_____
_____
_____
_____

12. Do you remember closing your heart (spirit) to either of your parents? In other words, did you lose basic trust?

_____
_____
_____
_____
_____
_____

13. How did you cope with your hurt (Withdrawal? Drugs? Anger? Striving? Performing to gain approval? Critical of others? Etc.?)

_____

_____

_____

_____

_____

_____

_____

14. What are your greatest areas of struggle today?

_____

_____

_____

_____

_____

_____

_____

15. Can you remember vowing not to do anything as the result of being hurt by your parents?

_____

_____

_____

_____

_____

_____

_____

Glossary of Terms

Abraham (Isaac and Jacob)—The physical and spiritual fathers of Israel; their direct descendants are the Jewish people.

Adoption—In the natural, adoption is the acceptance of another person's child as one's own. In the spiritual, individuals are made to be God's adopted sons and daughters when they receive Jesus as their personal Lord and Savior.

Apostle—An individual who functions in God's family as a spiritual father, a trainer and equipper, and church planter. Apostles are primarily concerned about establishing foundations so the church can be built properly upon Christ.

Authority—The God-given power to build others up for their blessing and benefit.

Bambino—The Spanish term for baby.

Baptism of the Holy Spirit—A spiritual experience when God reveals Himself to a person as Father. The main evidence of this experience is speaking in tongues—but also includes prophesying (see Acts 19:6).

Bar Mitzvah—Son of the commandments.

Blessing—When God presents to you a gift on bended knee. It also means multiplication as God heaps His favor upon your life!

Comforter—The third Person of the Trinity or Holy Spirit.

Confession—To agree with God and others that you have sinned.

Curse—When your health, finances, etc., are steadily stripped away.

Covenant—An agreement, treaty, oath, or promise established in blood (i.e., Christ's blood on the cross).

Elijah—An Old Testament prophet who served God and the nation of Israel.

Elijah House—A counseling center in Washington state where people go for inner healing.

Elisha—The protégé of Elijah; also an Old Testament prophet.

Forgiveness—When an individual chooses not to hold an offense committed against him by another person.

God's glory—God's manifest presence.

Grace—God's undeserved favor.

Grafted in—The process of being spiritually connected to God's chosen people, the Jews.

Holy Spirit—The Spirit of God.

Identificational Repentance—Identificational repentance is a term coined by John Dawson to describe a type of prayer which identifies with and confesses before God the sins of one's nation, city, people group, church, or family within the context of father-mother heart healing.[1] Identificational repentance takes place when someone stands in the place of a parent and confesses to a child or adult any way they did not carry them in their heart.

Iniquity—The presence of twistedness within an individual or family—literally to make crooked or pervert.

Inner Vow—An inner directive made subconsciously with an individual's mind, will, and emotions to protect themselves from future pain.

In Utero—In a woman's uterus, before birth; emotional wounds sustained during pregnancy.

Janteloven Stronghold—Ten laws that govern the way Scandinavian and other societies function.

Legalism—A law-oriented perspective that gives little or no room for others to fail.

Orphan—According to Jack and Trisha Frost, an orphan is someone who "does not have a safe and secure place in God the Father's heart. He feels no place of affirmation, protection, comfort, belonging, or affection. Self-oriented, lonely and inwardly isolated, he has no one from whom to draw Godly inheritance. Therefore, he has to strive, achieve, compete, and earn everything he gets in life. It easily leads to a life of anxiety, fears, and frustration."[2]

Orthodox Jew—Orthodox Judaism is a branch of Judaism. Orthodox Jews religiously keep the Sabbath, eat Kosher foods, dress modestly, and are strict adherents to the 613 laws contained in the first five books of the Old Testament.

Parental Inversion—Occurs when a young man or woman steps into the role of parent because one of their parents has left a void in the family due to divorce, premature death, abandonment, etc. Parentally inverted individuals are normally overly responsible individuals who believe everything will fall apart unless they hold everyone up.

Passover—The first of three major feasts on the Jewish calendar (Passover, Pentecost, Tabernacles).

Pharisees—The Pharisees were a prominent "sect" of the Jews in the first century A.D.

Rejection—When an individual believes that he is not being accepted or perceives that he has been cast aside.

Renunciation—To renounce something means to "break ties" with the devil.

Repentance—Repentance is a change of mind prompted by a change of heart, resulting in personal transformation.

Revelation—An epiphany, revealing or disclosure through active or passive communication with God.

Spirit of Elijah—One of thirty names for the Holy Spirit listed in the Bible; a divine empowerment that restores parents to their children and vice versa.

The Fear of Man—A spiritual assignment that tries to intimidate others so they will run from or quit what they are doing.

The One New Man—The entire family of God in Christ (both Jews in Messiah and Gentiles in Christ).

Torah Scroll—A Torah scroll contains the first five books of the Old Testament.

Works—Trying to earn God's favor through acts of service and obedience.

Yarmulke—A small cap that Jewish men wear to remind themselves that God's hand is upon their lives.

Endnotes

Words for the Hawaiian Islands

1. Chad Taylor, "A Word to the Hawaiian Islands," prophetic word, June 3, 1999, *Consuming Fire*, http://www.consumingfire.com/hawaii.htm (accessed September 6, 2014).

2. Jack Frost and Tricia Frost, "In 1999—Six Waves of Love Across the Nations," prophetic word, *The Elijah List*, http://www.elijahlist.com/words/display_word/578 (accessed September 6, 2014).

Chapter Two
Understanding the Orphan Stronghold

1. "Marilyn Monroe," *Wikipedia*, last modified September 4, 2014, http://en.wikipedia.org/wiki/Marilyn_Monroe (accessed September 7, 2014).

2. "Mike Tyson," *Wikipedia*, last modified September 3, 2014, http://en.wikipedia.org/wiki/Mike_Tyson (accessed September 7. 2014).

3. "Mike Tyson Timeline (Parts 1 and 2)," About Sports, *About.com 2014*, http://boxing.about.com/od/records/a/tyson_timeline_2.htm (accessed September 7, 2014).

4. "Mike Tyson Biography," *Bio*, http://www.biography.com/people/mike-tyson-9512980#early-life (accessed September 7, 2014).

5. "Mike Tyson," *Wikipedia*.

6. "Lindsay Lohan," *Wikipedia*, last modified September 4, 2014, http://en.wikipedia.org/wiki/Lindsay_Lohan (accessed September 7, 2014).

7. Ibid.

8. Ibid.

9. Lindsay Lohan, "Confessions of a Broken Heart (Father to Daughter) Lyrics," Lindsay Lohan Lyrics, *Metrolyrics 2013 CBS Interactive*, Inc., http://www.metrolyrics.com/confessions-of-a-broken-heart-daughter-to-father-lyrics-lindsay-lohan.html (accessed September 6, 2014).

Chapter Three
How Do We Get Orphaned?

1. "Defeating the Orphan Spirit through Godly Belief Systems," five charts, Living Water Christian Fellowship, xa.yimg.com/kq/groups/16421723/623710089/name/The (accessed September 7, 2014).

2. Jack Frost, *Experiencing Father's Embrace* (Shippensburg, PA: Destiny Image, 2002), 113–120.

3. Ibid.

Chapter Four
Recognizing the Orphan Within Us!

1. Jack Frost and Trisha Frost, "From Slavery to Sonship (2)," page 2, *Shiloh Place Ministries*, http://www.shilohplace.org/wp-content/uploads/2013/12/slavery-to-sonship-2-jack-and-trisha-frost_20081231-093411.pdf (accessed September 10, 2014).

Chapter Five
My Father! My Father!

1. Nathan Stone, *Names of God in the Old Testament* (Chicago: Moody Press, 1944), 34.

2. Jeff A. Brenner, "The Aaronic Blessing," Hebrew Research Center, *Ancient Hebrew Research Center*, http://www.ancient-hebrew.org/12_blessing.html (accessed September 7, 2014).

3. Ibid.

Chapter Six
Breaking Free from the Orphan Stronghold

1. Jack Frost, *Experiencing Father's Embrace*, 113-120.

2. "The Father's Blessing," *Shiloh Place Ministries*, https://www.shilohplace.org/shop/products/the-fathers-blessing-bookmark/# (accessed September 8, 2014).

Chapter Nine
Divine Relating: The Key to Raising Healthy Children

1. John Sandford and Paula Sandford, *Healing the Wounded Spirit* (Tulsa, OK: Victory House, 1985).

Chapter Ten
Different Ways Parents Unintentionally Wound Their Children

1. Sandford, *Healing the Wounded Spirit*, 40–42.

Chapter Twelve
Ejection of Rejection

1. *The Free Dictionary*, s.v. "reject," http://www.thefreedictionary.com/reject (accessed September 9, 2014).

2. Ibid.

Chapter Thirteen
A Dad's Job Description

1. Perry Stone, *Breaking the Jewish Code* (Lake Mary, FL: Creation House, 2009), 217–220.

Chapter Fourteen
Reaching Your God-Given Potential is Possible

1. "Marianne Williamson," *Wikipedia*, last modified September 7, 2014, http://en.wikipedia.org/wiki/Marianne_Williamson (accessed September 9, 2014).

2. Marianne Williamson, *A Return to Love: Reflections on the Principles of a Course in Miracles* (New York: HarperCollins, 1992).

3. "Law of Jante," *Wikipedia*, last modified August 14, 2014, http://en.wikipedia.org/wiki/Law_of_Jante (accessed September 9, 2014).

4. Ibid.

5. *Academic Dictionaries and Encyclopedias*, s.v. "Mosaic," (Mosaic Law, moseloven) http://translate.enacademic.com/mosaic/en/no/1 (accessed September 9, 2014).

6. "Law of Jante," *Wikipedia*.

7. "Japanese Proverbs," *Wikipedia*, last modified September 7, 2014, http://en.wikipedia.org/wiki/Japanese_proverbs (accessed September 9, 2014).

8. "Tall Poppy Syndrome," *Wikipedia*, last modified September 4, 2014, http://en.wikipedia.org/wiki/Tall_poppy_syndrome (accessed September 9, 2014).

9. Susan Page, "Hawaii's Oppression by Mediocrity," *Midweek*, June 1, 2005, http://archives.midweek.com/content/columns/susanspage_article/hawaiis_oppression_by_mediocrity/.

Chapter Fifteen
Transforming Our Land One Family at a Time

1. "The Blind Side (film)," *Wikipedia*, last modified September 4, 2014, http://en.wikipedia.org/wiki/The_Blind_Side_ (film) (accessed September 9, 2014).

Chapter Seventeen
Restoring Our Hearts to Our Jewish Fathers

1. "Alex Haley," *Wikipedia*, last modified August 25, 2014, http://en.wikipedia.org/wiki/Alex_Haley (accessed September 9, 2014).

2. "After 1,878 Years Israel Becomes a Nation Again May 14, 1948," *Examiner.com*, http://www.examiner.com/article/after-1-878-years-israel-becomes-a-nation-again-may-14-1948 (accessed September 12, 2014).

3. Rob Gross, *Legacy of Blessing* (Kapolei, HI: White Mountain Castle, 2009), 32–33.

Glossary of Terms

1. John Dawson, *Healing America's Wounds* (Ventura, CA: Regal, 1994).

2. Jack Frost and Trisha Frost, "From Slavery to Sonship (2)," page 3.

About the Author

Pastor Rob Gross planted Mountain View Community Church in 1992 in Kaneohe, Hawaii, and continues to serve as senior pastor, along with his wife Barbara. He develops pastors who minister in other churches and spends time equipping God's people for Kingdom service. He is known as a pastor to pastors and has a prayer-counseling ministry known for releasing breakthrough and healing in people's lives. He has taught workshops and seminars about the Gifts of the Spirit, Prophetic Evangelism, The One New Man, The Feasts of Israel, The Sabbath, The Orphan Stronghold, and The Father's Blessing.

Rob grew up in Kaneohe and is of Jewish and Japanese ancestry. He graduated from Iolani High School and earned his bachelor's degree and Phi Beta Kappa honors from the University of Hawaii. After working five years in the marketplace, he earned his master of divinity degree from Golden Gate Baptist Theological Seminary. He has ministered throughout the United States and countries such as Ireland, Japan, and Thailand. From 1997–2002 he led The Watch of the Lord—a multidenominational monthly intercessory gathering that petitioned the Lord for revival in the Hawaiian Islands. In 2001 he helped launch 96744 United in Prayer and has served on the board of 808 United in Prayer. He has also served as chaplain of the Castle Varsity baseball team for eight years. Rob has been married for 30 years to his wife, Barbara, and has three adult sons, Jordan (and daughter-in-law Stephanie), Brandon, and Jonathan.

Contact the Author

Visit the author's website at:

www.familylegacyinternational.org.

Made in United States
Orlando, FL
13 May 2022